THE LITTLE LIBRARY PARTIES

Kate Young is an award-winning food writer, cook and bookworm. Her Little Library Cookbooks (*The Little Library Cookbook, The Little Library Year*, and *The Little Library Christmas*) feature food inspired by famous, beloved and occasionally obscure works of literature. She has written about food, books, and sexuality for various publications, including the *Guardian, Prospect Magazine, Slightly Foxed, Stylist, Delicious*, and *Sainsbury's Magazine*. After a sunny Australian childhood, spent indoors reading books, she moved to London, which suited her much better. She is now based in the English countryside. You can follow her on Twitter and Instagram (@bakingfiction).

Yuki Sugiura is an award-winning London-based photographer and director, specializing in food, interiors, people and travel. Originally from Japan, she studied ceramics and graphic design at Camberwell Art College. She photographs for newspapers, magazines and book publishers, and also works on advertising campaigns for lifestyle companies and food retailers. Recent editorial clients include Martha Stewart, the *Financial Times, Bon Appétit*, the *Guardian, House & Garden* and *The New York Times T Magazine*.

THE LITTLE LIBRARY PARTIES

50 recipes to share with friends

KATE YOUNG

an Apollo Book

First published in 2022 by Head of Zeus Ltd,
part of Bloomsbury Publishing Plc

Copyright © Kate Young, 2022
Photography © Yuki Sugiura, 2022

1 3 5 7 9 10 8 6 4 2

A catalogue record for this book is available from
the British Library.

ISBN
9781803281230 (TPB)
9781803281223 (E)

Design by Jessie Price
Photography by Yuki Sugiura

Printed in 2022 by L.E.G.O. S.p.A.

Head of Zeus Ltd
5–8 Hardwick Street
London EC1R 4RG
www.headofzeus.com

*For everyone in the kitchen at parties
(and most especially for Ella)*

PARTIES

August is quickly realizing that it's only a brunch in the absolute loosest definition of the word: there is brunch food, yes, and Isaiah introduces her to a Montreal queen hot off a touring gig with a fistful of cash and a Nalgene full of mimosas. But, mostly, it's a party.

One Last Stop, Casey McQuiston

There's an episode of *The Simpsons* I think about a lot – that perfect one where Kirk Van Houten stands pointing at a potato-shaped blob on a sheet of Pictionary paper shouting 'Dignity, it's dignity!' It starts with Marge and Homer in bed one night. Book in her lap, unsettled and rigid with anxiety, Marge asks Homer if this is how he imagined married life. He seems content, but she is questioning things – she pictured cocktail parties and candlelit dinners. She pictured napkins. And so she decides to host a party.

I get it. I spent my childhood picturing napkins and dinners and parties. Before school, around the breakfast table, I'd pull Mum's cookbooks from the shelf, and plan imaginary menus for the dinners I'd host once I was older. Perhaps something with aubergine and tahini and pomegranates from Claudia Roden's *Arabesque* to start, then one of Stephanie Alexander's lamb chop recipes, and Nigella Lawson's perfect clementine and almond cake to finish. Or maybe something low-key, like that peach, mint and prosciutto salad from one of Jamie Oliver's books, and then an ice cream I'd make myself in my shiny machine. For a fancy birthday I'd serve oysters (I didn't like them yet, but was convinced it was only a matter of time), Julia Child's bœuf bourguignon, and some buttery French tart from the patisserie on the other side of Brisbane. People would bring wine and flowers and compliments. I'd light candles. I'd bring out the good linen serviettes, write place cards, and polish those crystal glasses I found in a market somewhere on holiday. I dreamed so longingly of being a grown-up that in many ways I wished away my teenage years, and the potential joys to be found therein.

It's a glorious relief that it appears I wasn't wrong to be eagerly anticipating this period of my life. I've reached the age I sort of always was in my head, old enough to finally fit inside my own skin. After a few years spent working for people in their houses, I now have a space of my own, one I can welcome my friends into. I have nice serviettes, and some crystal glasses that once belonged to my great grandad, and some plates I found in a market somewhere on holiday. I have my own collection of cookbooks, and I sit with them when dreaming up parties and events.

When I was planning this book, I had a long conversation with my friend Berta about that point at which 'coming round for dinner' morphs into a dinner party. Semantics matter when we talk. Berta spoke Spanish and Italian before she spoke English, and so she's not lazy or vague or euphemistic with language (unless she plans to be). She says what she means. We agreed that there is a distinction – that there's something about a party that feels different. But it was hard to name, to find the shape of it. Why is it, we wondered, that the brunch in *One Last Stop* is a party and not a brunch, and why do we know immediately what that implies?

Like the best man with scuffed note cards giving a speech, I'm afraid I'm going to tell you that the Collins English Dictionary defines a party as 'a social event, often in someone's home, at which people enjoy themselves doing things such as eating, drinking, dancing, talking, or playing games'. It's so vague. Like the dictionary definition of love, or family, trying to affix a definitive label fails on so many counts. It captures nothing of the energy of a party. It does nothing to distinguish between brunch or dinner and a party – nothing to highlight that magical tipping point.

In the end, Berta and I landed on washing up: at a party, the host washes up once everyone has gone home. It's not quite that simple, I suppose; sometimes at a party my friends are pushy and pick up a sponge before I can talk them out of it. But a party is an event, an evening of note, even if you're welcoming close friends. What follows here, then, are fifty recipes for parties: for parties in the garden on long summer evenings, for house parties in crowded living rooms, for cosy dinner parties, for glamorous weddings, for quaint tea parties with dainty crockery (or a collection of mismatched mugs and a plate, if that's more your speed). For occasions and events worth celebrating.

You can celebrate on your own, of course, with one other person, or with just a handful. I know this intimately: I live alone and have spent much of these far-from-roaring twenties celebrating things – birthdays, publication dates, babies, friends falling in love, new jobs, promotions, Tuesdays – in all sorts of assorted groups. I've celebrated with one friend on the end of the telephone, and with groups of us outdoors on distanced picnic blankets. I'm not negating those more intimate guest lists, but most of the recipes here are for a few of you, or more. There are no recipes for one, though I have eaten plenty of these dishes alone – and then again the next day. Things can be scaled up, or down. But the general rule for all these dishes is that they're designed to be shared.

In one of his *Observer* columns (it was 2005, to place things in context), Nigel Slater claimed that the only people hosting dinner parties anymore were gay couples and antique dealers. I would have been devastated at seventeen – I didn't yet know I was gay and might be afforded a special dinner party pass. But, if Nigel Slater is as correct as he always is, then this book is for the gay couples and the antique dealers... and for everyone else who loves to have friends round. I do so hope you enjoy it.

NOTES ON RECIPES

Unless otherwise stated, when testing these recipes, all eggs were large, all butter was salted, and all milk was whole.

My oven is an electric oven. Unless I note otherwise, I use it without the fan. If your oven has a fan, then you will need to drop the stated oven temperature by between 15 and 20 degrees. In general, you know your oven best; keep an eye on things as the listed cooking time comes to an end.

I shop at my local market, butcher, fishmonger, greengrocer and supermarkets in Gloucestershire. Inevitably, though, I have less access to ingredients than I did when I lived in London. If hunting for a specific ingredient that my local shops don't stock, I will generally turn to online suppliers like SousChef or The Fish Society.

GARDEN PARTIES

There's a touch of nineteenth-century England in every garden party. In England the skies are hardly ever clear, but when at last the balmy summer days do arrive, the lords and ladies hold these sorts of semiformal parties on their country estates.

'Aloeswood Incense' from *Love in a Fallen City*, Eileen Chang

There is something distinctly English about the garden parties I have in my head. Before I moved here, Australians would pull me aside to warn me about the rain, about the grey skies and clouds they'd seen on their trips, about the drizzly January days. It's a narrative that's impossible to escape when you're leaving the sun-soaked southern hemisphere for this somewhat less temperate isle. But I knew about England already – I'd spent a winter in London when I was at university, determined to prove to myself that I could hack it. Back then, I was pleased to be able to reassure everyone that I loved the cold and the rain, that I was an indoor winter girl, that England would suit me just fine. A decade and a bit on, I mostly stand by it.

But when the sun is out in England, as she so often is, when the sky is a pale cloudless blue, when the world smells like mown grass and elderflower and honey, it's incomparably lovely. It's Sebastian and Charles drinking Champagne on the lawn at Brideshead; it's Mary and Colin and Dickon in the secret garden once it has begun to bloom again, it's Austen's Dashwoods sitting in the grass with Willoughby, and Emma Woodhouse heading off with her friends to eat strawberries; it's the play-going guests in Woolf's *Between the Acts* eating sandwiches and drinking lemonade; it's Winnie-the-Pooh and the inhabitants of the Hundred Acre Wood celebrating Eeyore's birthday; it's the hobbits gathered together for Bilbo's one-hundred-and-eleventh birthday. As Eileen Chang noted, there's a touch of nineteenth-century England, or at least the one I know from literature, about a garden party.

But there's a divide that exists here between those people who have the space to throw parties in their gardens, and those who quite simply don't. Natasha Brown's brilliant debut, *Assembly*, is about garden parties that are exclusive, that feel inaccessible, that speak of the sort of white, privileged England that benefits only a few (often including, to be clear, me). These parties hark back to country estates, to colonialism, and to staff who eased the way between the kitchen and the picnic blanket.

My experience of England is mostly of an England without gardens; the majority of my homes here have been flats with no outdoor space. Our outdoor culture is not as ingrained as it is in (say) Australia – there is no democratization of outdoor space, few publicly accessible barbecues, insufficient public toilets. I've been lucky to have generally had walking-distance access to good parks, spaces to lay out picnic rugs and bring out food. But there's a reason that garden parties here retain a sense of being slightly posher than I am – slightly out of reach. And so I want to advocate for reclaiming garden parties from the nineteenth century, for all of us this time, and even in the absence of a garden of your own. For setting up in a corner of your local park, for finding somewhere to light a disposable barbecue, for throwing the windows open, spreading a picnic rug on the floor in a patch of sun, and breathing in the summer.

There are fifteen different sandwich options served in Katherine Mansfield's *The Garden Party*, which should be enough to convince you of just how wonderfully appropriate they are for an outdoor party: they're portable, simple and adaptable. Plus, the mere act of slicing them into fingers is a veritable magic trick – one that turns sandwiches from soggy lunchbox fodder into a fancy little snack that can be served on a tray with a cup of tea or a glass of fizzy wine.

Mum used to make them in bulk for events, ordering bread sliced lengthways from the bakery so she lost less bulk from crust off-cuts. But for a little gathering in a garden, a supermarket loaf will suffice. There are endless options for what to put between your bread slices: crunchy rounds of cucumber with white vinegar, white pepper and cress; thinly sliced ham with hot English mustard; smoked salmon and cream cheese with black pepper and a spritz of lemon. But despite my love of the familiar, I'm always on the hunt for a new favourite. Happily, Mansfield delivers: she mentions an egg and tapenade filling. I've yet to come across an egg sandwich I don't like, but these are particularly special.

EGG AND TAPENADE FINGER SANDWICHES

Makes 6 rounds or 18 fingers (easy to scale up for a bigger event)

TAPENADE
120g (1¼ cups) pitted kalamata olives
5 anchovy fillets
1tbsp capers
1 garlic clove
2tsp red wine vinegar
2tbsp olive oil
Sea salt and black pepper

SANDWICHES
8 eggs at room temperature
4tbsp mayonnaise
12 slices white bread
Butter at easy spreading temperature

1. Make the tapenade first; you can do this up to a couple of days in advance if that's easier. With a stick blender or food processor, blitz

your olives with the anchovies, capers and garlic. Add the vinegar, and then the olive oil in a thin stream, until the tapenade comes together in a paste. Taste for seasoning – it's unlikely to need salt, but you may like to add a little extra vinegar, as well as some pepper. Scoop the tapenade into a pot and cover it with a layer of oil if you're planning to store it.

2. Bring a pot of water to the boil and, once simmering, lower the eggs into it. Set a timer for 8 minutes. When the timer pings, run the eggs under plenty of cold water until they're cool enough to comfortably hold. Peel the eggs and finely chop. Mix with the mayonnaise and season to taste.

3. To assemble, take two slices of bread, spreading one very thinly with butter, and the other with tapenade. Spoon some of the egg mix over the butter, and push it out to the edges. Put the tapenade slice over the top and then trim the crusts off. Slice the sandwich into equal thirds (or four long fingers – depending on how wide your loaf is).

Set at the brink of war, in the garden of an English stately home, Virginia Woolf's final novel, *Between the Acts*, exists between the play that is being staged in the garden and the party that accompanies it. Bubbling under the surface of the lightness and frivolity is a dread of the inevitable. But, in the meantime, there are sandwiches and the late afternoon sun. Lucy Swithin, to whom the responsibility of everything being ready seems to fall, bustles around the kitchen and the garden, casting her eye over the events before sending the food outside.

The sandwiches, 'some neat, some not', seem to be filled with ham, but there's also been a delivery from the fishmonger, so I'm taking liberties. Smoked salmon sandwiches are an undeniable joy, but I love these too: tender flakes of poached salmon alongside crisp spring vegetables, with just enough sharp homemade mayonnaise to prevent it all from falling out. Everything below is a suggestion, obviously – play around with what works for you in terms of the salad vegetables. It's a sandwich; it's very difficult to get this wrong.

POACHED SALMON SANDWICHES

Makes 6 rounds or 18 fingers (easy to scale up for a bigger event)

MAYONNAISE
2 egg yolks
1tbsp lemon juice
300ml (1¼ cups) neutral oil
1tsp hot English mustard

SANDWICHES
250g (9oz) poached salmon*
A dozen sugar snap peas, finely sliced
A handful of freshly podded peas – or
    pour boiling water over frozen ones
Leaves from 8 fronds of dill
12 slices brown or seeded bread

*This is a lovely use for any leftover salmon from the dish on p128, or for tinned poached salmon. If you want to poach your own, bring 300ml/1¼ cups milk to a simmer with 10 whole peppercorns and a bay leaf. Turn off the heat, place 250g/9oz fresh salmon in the milk, cover and leave it to poach in the hot liquid for 10 minutes.

1. For the mayonnaise, first ensure your ingredients and bowl are at room temperature. Whisk the egg yolks in a small bowl and then whisk in the lemon juice. Whisk constantly as you slowly drip the oil into the bowl. Keep it slow and steady. If the mayonnaise threatens to split, or looks like it has, add a teaspoon of boiling water and whisk vigorously to bring it back together. Either way, don't panic and keep it slow. Continue until the mayonnaise is thick and holds its shape when you move a whisk through it. Season with the mustard.

2. Flake the salmon and put in a bowl with the sliced sugar snaps, the peas and the dill. Gently fold through enough mayonnaise to hold everything together. Be gentle with it – the flakes of salmon should be as generous as possible, rather than mashed.

3. To assemble the sandwiches, take two slices of bread and open them in front of you. Scrape a little mayonnaise over both sides, and then place a few spoons of the filling in the centre of one of the slices. Place the other on top, and slice as you prefer – into halves with the crusts, or fingers with the crusts trimmed.

Early in the school year, before Bunny goes over the edge, the group at the centre of *The Secret History* spend their weekends at Francis's house. The October days are unseasonably warm, and they spend them outdoors. There are lazy games of tennis and croquet, long books to read, boats to drift in, and Bloody Marys to drink. And there are occasional picnics too, ambitious ones with 'elaborate menus' and martinis kept cold in thermoses.

The contents of the picnic basket are left for us to imagine, but it's clear the plates are porcelain rather than plastic – a fancier picnic than I'm used to preparing. I decided it called for something seasonal and portable – a tart, then, filled with one of my top-tier October vegetables, the ones always in my shopping trolley: Brussels sprouts. It's perfect with a martini from a thermos; I promise I've tested this extensively.

A FANCY AUTUMNAL TART

Serves 6–8

PASTRY

200g (1½ cups) plain (all-purpose) flour, plus extra for dusting
1tsp fennel seeds, finely ground
A pinch of fine salt
100g (3½oz) cold butter, cut into cubes
1 egg, beaten with 1tbsp cold water

FILLING

250g (9oz) Brussels sprouts, cleaned, stems cut off, and shredded
½ fennel bulb, very finely sliced
2tbsp flavourless oil
2 eggs
200ml (scant 1 cup) double (heavy) cream
A pinch of salt
1tbsp chopped tarragon
100g (3½oz) Taleggio cheese, in slices

1. Make the pastry first – you need to start this a couple of hours before you want your tart ready, as it needs plenty of resting time. Mix the flour, fennel seeds and salt in a bowl, then use your fingertips to rub in the butter (this is even easier in a food processor, if you have one). Use half the egg and water mix to bring the pastry together into a

dough. Try not to overwork it at this stage. Shape the dough into a disc, wrap it in plastic wrap and rest it for an hour in the fridge.

2. Roll the pastry out on a lightly floured surface until it's the thickness of a pound coin, then lower it into a 22cm (8½in) loose-bottomed tart pan. Press the pastry firmly into the fluted sides, patch any cracks or gaps, and prick the base all over with a fork. Leave the overhang; we'll be trimming it after we blind bake the tart. Return to the fridge for another hour.

3. Heat the oven to 200°C/400°F/Gas 6. Line the tart shell with greaseproof paper and fill with baking beans or uncooked rice. Bake for 20 minutes, then remove the paper and beans, trim the pastry overhang with a sharp knife and paint the tart shell with the rest of the beaten egg. Return to the oven for 8–10 minutes, until golden.

4. While the pastry bakes, prepare the filling. Fry the Brussels sprouts and fennel in the oil for 15 minutes, until golden and soft. You don't want the vegetables to be crisp or charred so keep the heat low. This tart is soft and gentle – everything *The Secret History* is not, really. Set aside to cool a little.

5. Whisk together the eggs and cream and stir in the salt and tarragon. Mix in the cooled vegetables, then pour the filling into the tart shell and push the Taleggio slices into the mixture. Turn the oven right down to 150°C/300°F/Gas 2 and bake the tart for 35–40 minutes, until golden on top and still wobbly in the middle. Serve at room temperature, with something fresh and bright alongside it – leaves with a sharp vinaigrette would be perfect, as would a carrot râpées.

On the longest day of the year, *I Capture the Castle*'s Cassandra Mortmain retreats to the wild gardens around the family home, lights a bonfire, and burns salt and sage. It's an annual sisterly ritual, but Rose is in London, and so it is only Héloïse the cat who keeps her company. Later, her beloved Simon (her sister's fiancée) will arrive as she is dancing around the flames, but before he does there is a ceremonial cake in the last light of dusk.

The cake itself is a take on a classic Swedish *Midsommar* one – a sponge made light with beaten egg whites and flavoured with the elderflowers that make summer smell so sweet and fragrant. Fresh strawberries and cream make this a poor cake for a picnic, I'm afraid, but a perfect one to pull from the fridge and bring into the garden at the last minute.

MIDSUMMER CAKE

Serves 8–10

CAKE
Butter, for greasing
6 eggs
225g (generous 1 cup) golden caster (superfine) sugar
3tbsp elderflower cordial
200g (1½ cups) plain (all-purpose) flour

FILLING
300ml (1¼ cups) double (heavy) cream
2tbsp elderflower cordial
400g (14oz) strawberries, hulled

TO DECORATE
Thyme, mint, edible flowers (optional)

1. Preheat the oven to 180°C/350°F/Gas 4. Grease and line two 20cm (8in) sandwich pans. Separate the eggs into two bowls and add the sugar and cordial to the yolks, then whisk until pale and smooth. Stir in the flour.

2. Beat the egg whites to stiff peaks and stir a third into the yolk mixture to loosen the batter. Gently fold in the remaining two-thirds, then divide the batter between the pans.

3. Transfer to the oven for 22–25 minutes, until the cakes are risen, golden and coming away from the sides of the pans. Remove the cakes from the oven and leave to cool for 5 minutes in their pans, then turn out onto a wire rack to cool completely.

4. For the filling, pour the cream and elderflower cordial into a clean bowl and beat by hand to very soft, billowy peaks. Go slowly towards the end, as it's so easy to over-mix and for the cream to split into butter (especially when the weather is warm).

5. Finally, layer up. Cut the larger strawberries into slices, keeping a handful of the prettiest whole for the top. Spread half the cream onto one of the cakes, top with the strawberries, and then place the other cake on top. Top with the rest of the cream, and decorate with the reserved strawberries and some thyme, mint and edible flowers, if using. Store in the fridge until you're ready to eat and then bring the cake out to the ceremonial bonfire. Serve in generous slices.

In the end they stopped looking for places because there were only spaces out here, and they found some mangy trees back off the road a way where they could make a fire, stretch some tarps from the car roof and fry sausages.

Cloudstreet, Tim Winton

Both my mum and dad have a barbecue on their back deck. They're not covered up and collecting dust either; a not-insignificant number of our meals growing up were cooked outdoors, meat and veg carried out from the kitchen to be placed over flames. Outside our house, we were never short of barbecuing opportunities either: Saturday sausage sizzles outside Bunnings (p25), where a cheerful bloke holding a pair of tongs would swap a dollar coin for a sausage in white bread, topped with soft onions and tomato sauce that we'd drip onto our t-shirts; summer holidays that required an early arrival at the beach, in order to snaffle a barbecue in the shade, a copy of the newspaper ready to employ in the often fruitless attempt to clear away the grease left behind by yesterday's cooks; Sundays spent at parties with family friends, sitting in our still-wet togs around tables overcrowded with bowls of potato salad, paper napkins, plastic plates and charred meat.

The thing about barbecues is that they're an event too. Even when they're portable and impromptu, little more than a tarp and a fire between a couple of trees, they're more than just a meal. Heading out for 'a barbie' implies the sort of food you'll be eating, certainly, but it also implies the environment, the nature of the thing. It's a meal, but it's also automatically a party. Most barbecues I grew up around took a while to get going, and so there was endless time for jumping in the pool, backyard cricket, and rounds of Uno with cards warped by chlorinated water and summer sun.

Years on, it's so often how I find myself recalling my far-away family and friends, and my childhood: parties in the glare of the afternoon sun; a bucket or paddling pool filled with stubbies of beer and fast-melting ice; vibrant salads passed back and forth in cheerful, bright plastic bowls; folding chairs set up in wide circles; damp beach towels thrown down and used as picnic blankets.

A few months before my beloved granddad died in 2006, my whole extended family returned to Brisbane for Christmas. We were dotted all over the country at that point – as distant from each other as London is from Istanbul – but knowing it would be the last Christmas we would all spend together brought us back to the same place. My cousins are mostly of similar ages, so the week we were together was a blast, filled with dinners and parties and board games and dips in the pool. The day after Boxing Day, in my mum's backyard, we decided to host a Jimmy Buffet-themed party, ostensibly for my uncle (a self-identifying Parrot Head), but actually for all of us. We went off in search of the perfect burger buns to make 'Cheeseburgers in Paradise', shaped the patties by hand, mixed up a huge jug of margaritas, found a limbo stick, and demanded that everyone arrive in floral shirts. In among the grief, and the dread at the fast-approaching inevitability on the horizon, we had a boozy, silly night – one I remember as our definitive barbecue.

If I close my eyes, and think back to Saturday mornings in Australia, I can almost smell the onions frying. The sausage sizzle is an Australian institution, an inextricable part of the national culture and identity – outside polling stations, at Bunnings Warehouse on Saturday mornings, at school fundraisers. Sausage sizzles are not only familiar, they're a given. They're a great way to cook for a few hundred people, but they're equally good when there are just a handful of you to feed. In Tim Winton's *Cloudstreet*, Rose, Fish, Quick and Harry string up a tarp between the car and a couple of trees and prepare this – I can't imagine a better (or simpler) outdoor meal.

SAUSAGE SIZZLE

Makes enough to see 6 of you through an afternoon of cricket in the park

9 brown onions
60ml (¼ cup) vegetable oil, plus extra for cleaning the barbecue
A generous pinch of sea salt
A dozen sausages – traditional pork or your favourite veggie ones

A loaf of servo bread*
A bottle of lager**

TO SERVE
Ketchup, mustard or barbecue sauce

*Servo bread is bread from the service station. Your favourite supermarket loaf will work well here.
**The beer is very much optional here, but if you want the authentic experience, you need to be drinking one while you hold the tongs and turn the sausages, pour a bit of it over the onions, and tell everyone within earshot that they'll be the best onions in the world. You won't be wrong.

1. Before you leave home, peel the onions and slice them into half-moons. If you have a microwave, toss the sliced onions into a plastic freezer bag, twist it loosely closed, and give them a blast on high for 2 minutes. If you don't have a microwave, don't worry, they'll just take a little longer on the hot plate.

2. Clean your barbecue hot plate really well – especially if you're using one in the park. Put it on a high heat, scrape it down and then pour some oil onto it. Rub the oil around with some scrunched-up newspaper, which will collect a lot of the grime everyone else has left behind.

3. Once your hotplate is clean, set it to a moderate heat, pour half the oil over it, and start to fry the onions. This will take a while and you can't rush it – you're aiming for soft and caramelized, so you're looking at 30–40 minutes. Once they've softened, add the rest of the oil, and a big pinch of salt. Keep them moving every now and then, and make sure they're not cooking too fast or burning. Find the coolest spot on the plate if you need them to slow down, and splash a bit of your beer over them to keep them from crisping up.

4. When the onions have started to look golden, and have cooked down significantly, push them to the side and throw the sausages on the hot plate. Poke them with a fork so they don't burst. Sizzle until charred, and cooked through – about 15 minutes – flipping them regularly to ensure they cook evenly.

5. Each person should grab a slice of bread, place it on a piece of paper towel, then place a sausage and a big pile of onions on top. Add whatever sauce you fancy, and try not to get any of it down your top.

A note: Obviously you can do all of this on your hob/stovetop back home – a heavy-bottomed cast-iron frying pan will be the best substitute for a public barbecue – but nothing can quite make up for the flavour remnants of a thousand other sausage sizzles.

This satay is what I made when my stomach began rumbling midway through Kevin Kwan's *Crazy Rich Asians* – Rachel and Nick's first night in Singapore is spent in the outdoor market, feasting on plates from a range of vendors, including the best satay Rachel has ever eaten. In a book filled with food I want to eat, this was high on the list.

I grew up eating satay in Brisbane, at home and at Baan Thai and My Thai just down the road. So when I travelled to Singapore, to the market where Rachel and Nick eat, it was the charred sticks and spiced sauce I picked up first. The base for this sauce exists in Stephanie Alexander's extraordinary *The Cook's Companion*, which was on the shelf of all the passionately food-obsessed families I spent time with (or was a part of) when I was growing up. Like so many of her recipes, it's how I've been making it since childhood, often without realising it.

CHICKEN SATAY

Serves 4 as a starter

MARINADE
2 shallots
4 garlic cloves
1 long red chilli
1tsp shrimp paste
1 lemongrass stalk
1tsp ground turmeric
1tsp ground cumin
1tsp ground coriander
2tbsp palm sugar
60ml (¼ cup) soy sauce
1tbsp fish sauce

500g (1lb 2oz) chicken thigh fillets, cut into chunks

SATAY SAUCE
1tbsp tamarind paste
1tbsp palm sugar
100g (3½oz) crunchy peanut butter
5tbsp coconut milk
1tbsp lime juice
1tsp soy sauce

EQUIPMENT
4 wooden skewers

1. Blitz the dry ingredients for the marinade together in a food processor or with a stick blender. Once you have a rough paste, add

the soy and fish sauces and blitz again (take care of/take off whatever you're wearing: this spatters and stains).

2. Put the chicken in a mixing bowl or freezer bag, pour the marinade over the top and mix it through until the chicken is covered. Leave in the fridge for at least an hour, or overnight if that's easier.

3. Soak the wooden skewers in cold water, so they won't char and catch fire when over the heat. To make the dipping sauce, whisk all the ingredients together vigorously, until the palm sugar is no longer in clumps. Taste the sauce – you may fancy more soy or more lime – and set aside.

4. Thread the marinated chicken onto the skewers, ensuring you don't squash it up too much, or it will cook unevenly. Cook over a moderate heat on the barbecue or in a heavy-bottomed pan on the hob/stovetop for about 10 minutes, turning occasionally until charred on all sides and cooked through. Serve immediately, with the sauce on the side.

I associate backyard barbecues with generous salads as much as I do meat over the flames. I was always squeezing one of the big vibrant plastic bowls we had between my knees in the back seat of the car as we headed off to someone's pool, someone's garden, someone's back deck. Everything at a barbecue tastes better alongside something fresh, crisp and full of flavour.

GREEK SALAD WITH ROASTED RED PEPPERS

Serves 6 as a side

2–3 red (bell) peppers
1 red onion, sliced into half-moons
3tbsp red wine vinegar
300g (10½oz) fresh tomatoes, cut into wedges or slices
½ cucumber
75g (2¾oz) lamb's lettuce (mâche)

10g (⅓oz) fresh oregano leaves
200g (7oz) feta cheese, crumbled
100g (1 cup) pitted kalamata olives
3tbsp capers
4tbsp olive oil
2tsp dried oregano
Salt

1. Cook the peppers on the barbecue (or in a dry, hot frying pan) until charred and blackened all over. Wrap in foil or plastic wrap while still hot – they'll sweat and their skins will be easier to peel off.

2. Meanwhile, toss the sliced onion with the vinegar and a pinch of salt, and leave to soften.

3. Put your tomatoes in your serving dish, season with salt and set aside – a little time will make them taste even better. Slice the cucumber in half lengthways, scoop the seeds out, and then slice into half-moons.

4. Rub the blackened skins from the peppers, then pull the stem and seeds out. Cut into generous slices.

5. To assemble the salad, toss the cucumber, lamb's lettuce, oregano leaves, feta, olives and capers through the tomatoes. Scoop the onion out of the vinegar bowl, give it a squeeze, and add this too.

6. Whisk the olive oil and dried oregano through the onion-y vinegar. Dress the salad with as much of it as you like, before tossing again.

A ZINGY SLAW

Serves 6 as a side

1 Savoy cabbage
Zest and juice of 2 lemons
A pinch of sea salt
2 carrots
60g (2oz) walnuts
5 spring onions (scallions), finely sliced
  on the diagonal
2 crisp eating apples
25g (1oz) coriander (cilantro), chopped

2tbsp chopped chives

DRESSING
2 garlic cloves, finely minced
1tbsp honey
1tbsp cider vinegar
2tsp hot English mustard
100g (½ cup) yoghurt

1. Slice the woody spines out of the cabbage and finely shred the leaves. Place in a bowl with the lemon zest and juice and salt. Give the cabbage a good squeeze, making sure the lemon is distributed throughout, as you want it to soften and pickle very lightly. Leave it in the bowl for at least 15 minutes.

2. Peel and then slice the carrots into fine julienne (I use a cheap julienne peeler I bought an age ago from Lakeland, which makes this a very fast job). Toast the walnuts in a dry pan and roughly chop.

3. To make the dressing, whisk together the garlic, honey, vinegar and mustard in the bottom of your serving bowl. Mix in the yoghurt.

4. Squeeze the cabbage to get rid of any excess water and add to the dressing along with the carrot and spring onions. Julienne or grate the apples down to their cores, and add them in too, tossing everything together so they don't brown. Add the coriander and chives and toss gently, then top with the toasted walnuts. Serve immediately.

Trent Dalton's *Boy Swallows Universe* is peppered with moments that ran through me with a visceral ache of homesickness. His characters eat potato scallops and drink Kirks Pasito (Pasito! My old favourite!), hunt out packets of Iced VoVos, and enjoy plate after plate of Vietnamese food in Mama Pham's – crabs cooked in salt and pepper and chilli, whole fish with lemongrass, and these generously filled fresh rolls I loved most as a kid (and still regularly order now).

The rolling here can be done in advance, if you like. But you can also present the ingredients on a platter in the centre of your table, and allow your guests to fold their own wrappers with all their favourite bits. My friend Alex hosted a party like that once, on an impossibly warm Queensland day, and I've replicated it often since.

SUMMER ROLLS

Makes 12 (but very easy to scale up)

150g (5½oz) firm tofu
1tsp caster (superfine) sugar
2tbsp dark soy sauce
1tbsp sesame oil
A nest of fine rice noodles
2 large carrots
½ cucumber
1 head of butter lettuce
A handful of coriander (cilantro) leaves
A handful of Thai basil leaves

A handful of mint leaves
12 large rice paper wrappers

DIPPING SAUCE
3tbsp fish sauce
1tbsp caster (superfine) sugar
3tbsp lime juice
1 bird's eye chilli, deseeded if you would
  like less heat
1 thumb of ginger, peeled and grated

1. Drain your tofu and then wrap in paper towels before gently pressing beneath a weight to remove any excess moisture. Pat the tofu dry and then cut into thick slices; too thin and you risk them falling apart. Dissolve the sugar in the soy sauce and sesame oil and then pour over the tofu to marinate. Leave for at least 30 minutes while you prep the rest of the filling ingredients (or refrigerate the tofu overnight).

2. Over a moderate heat on the barbecue, or in a heavy-bottomed pan on the hob/stovetop, cook the tofu on both sides until caramelized, then set aside to cool completely (don't wrap it into the summer rolls while still warm – it will make everything sweat!).

3. Cover the rice noodles with boiling water and, once softened, drain and set aside. Lay all the other ingredients for the rolls out on your work surface; summer rolls are all about *mise en place*, so take some time to slice the carrots and cucumber into julienne, wash the lettuce leaves, and pull herbs from their stalks. Fill a bowl with cold water to soften the rice paper wrappers in.

4. To make the rolls, soften a wrapper for a minute or so, squeeze it dry and spread it out on your work surface. Wrap a few bits of carrot and cucumber in a lettuce leaf along with a small pile of the softened noodles. Don't worry if the lettuce breaks – you're just trying to keep everything more or less together. Place this on the lower edge of the wrapper. About halfway up, lay a slice of tofu, and add a couple of leaves of each herb. Roll the wrapper up and over the lettuce bundles, and then fold over the tofu and herbs. Fold the sides of the wrapper in, and then roll up to the top edge. Continue with the rest of the wrappers.

5. Whisk the ingredients for the dipping sauce together, taste, and serve with the rolls. The rolls will hang about in the fridge for a bit if you want to prepare them a few hours before serving, but do eat them while the filling is crisp and fresh.

Away Laura flew, still holding her piece of bread and butter. It's so delicious to have an excuse for eating out of doors, and besides, she loved having to arrange things; she always felt she could do it so much better than anybody else.

The Garden Party, Katherine Mansfield

As a party approaches I often wonder whether my enjoyment lies more in the arranging of things, than in the event itself. When I was young, planning certainly seemed to be the great joy of it – working out what sort of party we wanted to host, discussing menus over breakfast before school, writing guest lists and schedules. Mum had a huge stack of scrap paper held together with a large bulldog clip; it was her planning book, and one of us would be sent to retrieve it from the pantry when there was a party on the horizon. Eventually, lists that we drew up would be pulled from it and stuck to the fridge, or slotted into her Filofax. But every party we hosted had at some point existed in that stack of paper, as nothing more than a collection of ideas and people and food and glassware.

I still love planning, in all its forms. New ideas make their way onto bits of paper or onto Excel spreadsheets. In among the work that exists on my desktop and in my spiral notebook, there are ideas for future books, for menus, for shopping lists, for plans with people who are coming to stay. There are ideas for parties. There is a long gap, inevitably, in those notebooks, in the plans I was making over the last couple of years. Shopping lists that were for dropping off on doorsteps rather than for enjoying together in person. A gap when we didn't have parties, when friends didn't come to stay. I was mostly alone, for much longer than I would normally choose to be, living vicariously through parties on the page.

During this time, I returned over and over to Mansfield's *The Garden Party*. It is, without a doubt, the best party in literature. I suppose you could argue with me, propose your own favourites, but I'm afraid this is the joy (the sheer privilege) of writing it down in a book: I get to make wide, sweeping statements about the 'best' things and get away with it. And anyway, I'm not sure it's possible to convince me I'm wrong. The party itself is brief on the page, sparse in detail once the guests arrive. But we see so much of the planning. There are fifteen different sandwiches. The weather is perfect: 'windless, warm, the sky without a cloud'. The roses understand that they're expected to impress, for it is a garden party – their time to shine. A marquee is erected. And then there are the cream puffs that arrive from Godber's, along with the story of a man who has been killed nearby.

The tone of the story shifts here – Laura's attention to the planning is coloured by the news. How are they supposed to have the party, when life insists on continuing (or ceases to continue entirely) outside of it? How can it be true that the roses are perfect and the weather is ideal and the passionfruit ices something special, when there is a man dead in the cottages below? And, of course, how can we, now, keep planning for good things when the world is constantly 'ending' on a loop. How can parties be important when there is so much else happening around us?

Reading it in the depths of lockdown, I texted a beloved friend (Ella Risbridger, whose books on food and on life I recommend wholeheartedly) the closing lines of *The Garden Party*. She replied – as she so often does, as we so often do when we talk – in exclamation points and capital letters. It was how I learned that it's her favourite story, and that they're her favourite lines, because she knows just how deeply true they are.

'Isn't life,' she stammered, 'isn't life—' But what life was she couldn't explain. No matter. He quite understood.

'Isn't it, darling?' said Laurie.

Life is all of it, all at once. So we should all fill up notebooks with parties, and then invite people around. It will be impossible, ever again, to take for granted quite how great a privilege and a joy it is.

DINNER
PARTIES

Will be marvellous. Will become known as brilliant but apparently effortless cook. People will flock to my dinner parties, enthusing 'It's really great going to Bridget's for dinner, one gets Michelin star-style food in a bohemian setting.' Mark Darcy will be v. impressed and will realise I am not common or incompetent.

Bridget Jones's Diary, Helen Fielding

Despite all those parties that I have hosted, all the many I have attended, all the hundreds I have spent time at on the page, whenever someone mentions dinner parties I think of blue soup and marmalade. I think of the panic of absolutely everything going wrong, of the impossible shopping list, of worrying whether your guests will get along, of the sleepless mid-week nights spent in the kitchen, of friends sitting waiting with empty plates, of the horrifying realization that not a single course is in any way edible. I can taste Bridget's slightly burnt orange slices, her sudsy Fairy-liquid velouté, her raw fondant potatoes. It's a glorious piece of comic writing, because it's so terribly, convincingly real.

The true tragedy of it is that Bridget got it wrong from the outset. Even if everything had gone perfectly, no one would think they were getting *Michelin star-style food in a bohemian setting*. They would think she spent most of her time in the kitchen, that they barely saw their beloved friend, that she looked harried when they did catch a glimpse of her, that the food was a bit fussy, that they didn't need that many veloutés, that they would rather have had a roast chicken. I would almost always rather a roast chicken (there's one on p71).

What I am saying is: don't overcomplicate things. If you want to prepare multiple courses, then do – but maybe make sure one is done entirely in advance, or bought from a shop. If you want to try some new recipes, then do – but maybe make sure you cook at least one familiar favourite, so you have some solid ground. Invite at least one Mark Darcy too, someone willing to don an apron and step into the kitchen if you need a last-minute hand. After years of doggedly trying to do everything myself, of martyring myself over dinner, it's been made abundantly clear to me that people simply love to feel useful. Let them. Make them feel good. If you (like me) struggle with asking for help, make a little list of Jobs for Helpers in advance so that you know you can say, 'Yes! I would love for you to set the table!' or 'Could you wash and tear up that lettuce for our salad?' And remember that you don't have to wait for them to notice you have slightly too much on your plate; just ask. Life will be better for it. I promise.

All that said, sometimes I just want to impress. I love to show off in the kitchen. I love feeding people something they've never tried before. On my 30th birthday, I invited my friends round for a meal I had spent the better part of two days preparing – a sort-of recreation of Babette's Feast (p51). I loved it. And so it is not for me to tell you not to be extravagant, not to spend a day in the kitchen. I am very much here to support and cheerlead this impulse. The two menus that follow (from *Still Life* and from *Babette's Feast*) will let you do just that. But I also want to make sure you know that there are options. And so the dishes in the second half of the chapter are simpler, less fancy: one course, or maybe two, rather than three. And I need you to know, too, that putting a chicken and some potatoes in the oven, pulling a tub of ice cream from the freezer, and gathering people around your table to bask in each other's company and toast your general brilliance is as complicated as throwing a dinner party ever needs to be.

Spanning much of the twentieth century, Sarah Winman's *Still Life* follows Ulysses and Evelyn and their friends, as their paths cross in Florence and London's East End. It's kind and warm and open-hearted, and the food is so delightfully present that I felt certain the author must love to eat as much as I do. In her acknowledgements, Winman credits Florence-based food writer Emiko Davies with teaching her about Italian food history, and consulting on the dishes in the book. Emiko generously shared her recipe (guided by Pellegrino Artusi's 1891 version) for *sformato di carciofi* – a dish mentioned in *Still Life* that was entirely new to me. According to Emiko, it's somewhat like a frittata, and not quite like a soufflé. It works with fennel, or cauliflower, but it's glorious with artichoke. However you label it, it's delicious. A perfect dinner-party starter.

ARTICHOKE FLANS

Serves 6

250ml (1 cup) milk
2 bay leaves
30g (2tbsp) butter, plus extra for greasing
2tbsp breadcrumbs
75g (1 cup) finely grated Parmesan – or a
    vegetarian alternative
30g (3¾tbsp) plain (all-purpose) flour
2 eggs, plus 1 egg yolk
5–6 artichoke hearts*
Flaky sea salt

TO SERVE
2 courgettes (zucchini)
Zest and juice of 1 lemon
1tbsp olive oil
2 stalks of basil, leaves picked and
    shredded

EQUIPMENT
6 ramekins, 8cm (3¼in) across
A large, high-sided baking dish in
    which the ramekins all fit

*If you can come by whole artichokes easily and cheaply, then trim them down to their tender centres, remove the choke, and simmer in salted water for 5 minutes before drying out completely. If you would have to spend a couple of quid on each artichoke (as I do), use a tin of artichoke hearts in brine, drained and patted dry.

1. Place the milk in a pan with the bay leaves and bring to a simmer. Remove from the heat and leave to infuse for at least 10 minutes.

2. Grease your ramekins with butter and preheat your oven to 180°C/350°F/Gas 4. Mix together the breadcrumbs and 1tbsp of the grated cheese, and then add a pinch to each ramekin, turning it round until the bread and cheese line the sides.

3. Make a béchamel. Melt the butter in a small saucepan, then stir in the flour. Cook for a couple of minutes (don't scrimp on time here; you want to cook the taste of the flour out). Remove the bay leaves from the milk, add a splash of it to the pan and whisk it in. Continue adding the milk, in gradual splashes, simmering it until you have a smooth, thick sauce. Remove from the heat and allow to cool a little.

4. Whisk in the whole eggs, and then the rest of the cheese. Use a food processor or stick blender to blitz the artichokes to a smooth purée and fold that into the mix. Season with a pinch of salt (the cheese is salty, but you do need more salt to lift this).

5. Distribute the mixture between your ramekins. Add a splash of water to the egg yolk in a little bowl, then whisk this with a fork and paint it onto the top of each flan. Place the ramekins in your baking dish, pour the water from a just-boiled kettle around them, and carefully transfer to the oven. Cook for 25–30 minutes until browned on top.

6. While they bake, ribbon your courgettes using a vegetable peeler. Place in a bowl with the lemon zest and juice, the olive oil and a pinch of salt, and toss through the basil leaves. Serve each ramekin on a plate with a handful of the salad.

Still Life's Ulysses hosts a party that we see only in its remnants. It's the kind of scene I love coming across, inviting us to imagine the meal that took place. The plates of anchovies and bowls of clams and beans that are strewn across the table make things simple here, easily reassembled into the dinner they once were.

This is such a great party dish. It's a bit messy, as any dish with shells is bound to be, so make sure you have some receptacles on the table for your debris, and plenty of serviettes for your fingers. Any leftover beans are delicious cold the next day, squashed onto a piece of toast drowned in olive oil. Do eat the clams on the day though (not that you need any encouragement) – they won't be nearly as nice after a night in the fridge.

BEANS WITH CLAMS

Serves 6

500g (1lb 2oz) whole fresh clams*
1tbsp olive oil
1 carrot, diced
2 celery sticks, diced
3 brown onions, 2 diced and 1 halved
3 garlic cloves, minced
3 sprigs of rosemary, leaves picked and finely chopped
1 x 400g (14oz) tin chopped tomatoes
500ml (2 cups) ham or chicken stock**

1 x 400g (14oz) tin borlotti beans
1 x 400g (14oz) tin cannellini beans
150ml (scant ⅔ cup) white wine
A big squeeze of lemon juice
Flaky sea salt

TO SERVE
6 slices ciabatta, or other crusty bread
3 garlic cloves, cut in half
100ml (scant ½ cup) olive oil

*If you can't find fresh clams, look for frozen ones. My local supermarket has cooked frozen clams still in their shells. Tip them in at the end, skipping the wine steaming altogether.
**I love ham stock here, which I occasionally have in the freezer (I save it after simmering a ham or ham hock). But chicken stock from a stock pot works too, and honestly you're – I'm – probably more likely to have it around.

1. When you arrive home with your clams, cover them in cold, salted

water (fresh water will kill them), and put them in the fridge until you're ready for them.

2. Warm the olive oil in a large saucepan, then gently fry the diced carrot, celery and onions until softened and fragrant. Add the garlic and cook for another couple of minutes. Add the rosemary and stir through, then pour in the chopped tomatoes. Half fill the empty tin with water, swirl it around and add the tomato-y water to the pan along with the stock.

3. Bring the contents of the pan to a simmer. Allow it to bubble slowly for about 40 minutes, becoming richer and more deeply flavoured. Give it a taste – it should be thick and fragrant with rosemary and garlic – if it isn't, give it a little more time (and a little more rosemary too, if you like). Season with salt.

4. Tip both tins of beans into a sieve, and run cold water over them. Tip them into the pan and simmer for a further 10 minutes.

5. Meanwhile, drain the clams, and discard any with broken shells. Add the wine and halved onion to a saucepan with a lid and bring to a simmer, then add the clams. Place the lid on, and give them a couple of minutes over a moderate heat, gently shaking occasionally. The clams should open in the steam – have a peek after 2 minutes.

6. Once the clams have opened, pull the onion out of the pan and discard, scoop the clams out and add to the beans, then strain the cooking liquor into the bean pot, and give everything a very good stir. Taste the beans again, adding perhaps more salt and certainly some lemon juice.

7. This will sit quite happily while you toast a slice of bread for each of you in a pan or under the grill. Rub each slice with a garlic clove half, and then dress with the olive oil and some more salt. Bring the beans and clams to the table and serve with the garlicky toasts in each bowl.

Stay with me here. I know that panforte is a Tuscan Christmas cake, and so probably entirely out of season alongside your artichoke flan and your clams and beans. In fact, it's Christmas Eve when Ulysses brings it out, so I can't even claim literary authenticity. That said, seasonality is merely a suggestion when it comes to this cake, and panforte is a glorious finale to a dinner party: ready entirely in advance, served in whatever portion size you have space for, perfect with a pot of coffee, ideal to linger over. It keeps for ages too, so you'll be able to enjoy the leftovers for a mid-morning snack.

This recipe is, I have to confess, a mere nod to the original in terms of its ingredients. But the thrill of a panforte is that it's so gloriously adaptable. What follows is my favourite version, but you can play around with nuts and fruit as you see fit. Panforte generally has a decent amount of candied peel in it, but if you're shopping in a supermarket you'll struggle to find any of the good stuff. If you find time to make your own, or can source any in a deli or online (I love candied pineapple, candied melon and candied orange peel) replace the 150g/5½oz dried fruit with them, and omit the orange zest.

PANFORTE

Serves at least 12

300g (10½oz) nuts – a mix of what you like, eg. almonds, pistachios, pine nuts
250g (9oz) sticky dried fruit, chopped – I like a mix of dates and figs here
150g (5½oz) dried fruit, chopped – I use dried apricots and cranberries
Zest of 3 oranges
175g (generous ¾ cup) caster (superfine) sugar
125g (generous ½ cup) honey
125g (4½oz) plain (all-purpose) flour

25g (¼ cup) cocoa powder
1tsp ground cinnamon
½tsp ground cardamom
½tsp ground coriander
½tsp ground black pepper
200g (scant 1½ cups) icing (confectioners') sugar

EQUIPMENT
Rice paper or greaseproof paper

1. Preheat the oven to 150°C/300°F/Gas 2. Grease and line a 20cm (8in) cake pan – traditional recipes use rice paper, and you should if you have some, but greaseproof paper is fine too. Toast the nuts in batches in a pan over a moderate heat (keep them separate, as the pine nuts will toast faster than the almonds). Keep an eye on them, and don't let them catch and burn, but do ensure they all get a lovely colour. Tip into a bowl, then add the chopped fruit and orange zest.

2. Put the sugar, honey and 100ml (scant ½ cup) water in a small saucepan and bring to a simmer. Heat to 115°C (239°F), or soft-ball stage. If you don't have a sugar thermometer, test by dropping a bit of the molten sugar into a glass of water; once cool you should be able to squidge the strands together into a malleable ball.

3. Stir the flour, cocoa powder and spices into the melted sugar and honey. Pour in the nuts and fruit and stir to combine. Press the filling into the prepared pan, then bake for 35 minutes. Remove from the oven and leave to cool in the pan, then turn out and cover with a generous layer of icing sugar.

When I turned thirty, I cooked Babette's Feast for a group of my closest friends. It's unusual to find a menu this detailed in a book – we're privy to everything, from the shopping list (a ten-day journey is made to place an order for ingredients from France) through the dinner party, and into the clean-up. It's clear Babette is a pro, a true master at work, a perfectionist when it comes to the art of dinner.

But, of course, the experience is a little different when you're both chef and birthday girl. Babette eschews the company of the guests and remains in the kitchen, but I wasn't hosting a supper club – I was having my friends around. And although many of the steps to follow can happen before the doorbell rings, some last-minute work and assembly is required. I say this not to put you off; the final tasks are all achievable while dressed in something fancy (though do put an apron on), and I have complete faith in you. To start then, an inauthentic non-yeasted blini, the work of minutes (not hours). Get a couple of your favourite guests into the kitchen with you for this. They can spoon out caviar while you flip blinis. Don't forget: no one wants you to martyr yourself, even for a dinner this delicious.

BLINIS NOT-DEMIDOFF

A generous starter for 6

2 whole eggs plus 1 egg yolk
300g (10½oz) cold mashed potato
150g (heaping 1 cup) plain (all-purpose) flour
1tsp baking powder
180ml (¾ cup) whole milk
A pinch of salt

Fronds from 8 sprigs dill
2tbsp butter

TO SERVE
150g (scant ⅔ cup) sour cream
Caviar or roe
Dill sprigs

1. Whisk the eggs and yolk into the cold mashed potato, then stir in the flour and baking powder. Whisk in the milk until you have a smooth batter. Season with salt and add the dill.

2. Melt a knob of the butter in a frying pan over a low-moderate heat and drop generous teaspoons of the batter in. When the tops of the blinis are covered with bubbles and are starting to look a little dry, flip them over. Cook the blinis in batches, adding more butter when the pan needs it, until all the batter is used up.

3. Serve each blini just barely warm (or the sour cream will melt off), with a dollop of sour cream, a little spoonful of caviar or roe, and a sprig of dill.

I'm not going to lie to you. These are a lot of work. They're for a dinner party when you're hoping to impress, when you want your guests to praise you as a genius and a goddess. You could make these for the fanciest of dinner companions and you'll knock their socks off. I lack Babette's humility (she steers clear of seeking praise in the dining room) and encourage you to cultivate a similar energy. Bask in the unparalleled glory of setting this down in front of your guests.

The dish in the book is *Cailles en Sarcophage*, invented by Babette in her Parisian restaurant. In the film we watch Babette prepare it; it's clear her recipe includes foie gras and black truffle and whole boned quails in their pastry cases. There are faithful recipes for it online. But when I first made this I was on a budget, and so this is my not-faithful version. Most importantly, you can get all the ingredients in a single trip to the supermarket. It's not quite as fancy, but I promise it will be just as impressive.

NOT-QUAILS EN SARCOPHAGE

Serves 6

PÂTÉ
45g (3tbsp) cold butter, cubed
1 shallot, finely chopped
125g (4½oz) cleaned chicken livers, diced
½tsp chopped thyme
2tbsp Armagnac or marsala
1tbsp double (heavy) cream
1tsp ground allspice
Sea salt and black pepper

PIES
750g (1lb 10½oz) all-butter puff pastry
2 eggs

LEEKS
2 thin leeks
150ml (scant ⅔ cup) chicken stock

1tbsp thyme leaves
2tbsp olive oil

SAUCE
20g (¾oz) dried porcini mushrooms
1tbsp butter
3 shallots, sliced
2 garlic cloves, minced
60g (2¼oz) chestnut mushrooms, diced
1tbsp plain (all-purpose) flour
3tbsp Armagnac or marsala
200ml (scant 1 cup) chicken stock
3tbsp double (heavy) cream

CHICKEN
2tbsp butter
6 boned chicken thighs, with skins on

1. First, make the pâté. Bring a tablespoon of the butter to a foaming heat in a frying pan over a moderate heat, then fry the shallot for 5 minutes until softened. Add the livers and thyme, and cook for a few minutes until the livers are browned on all sides, but still a little pink in the centre – cut one open to check.

2. Spoon everything into a food processor, but keep the frying pan on the heat. Add the alcohol to the pan and simmer away for a couple of minutes. Turn off the heat.

3. Whizz up the livers to a paste. Pour in the alcohol from the pan, along with the cream, allspice and a good pinch of salt and black pepper. With the food processor running on low, drop the remaining butter in piece by piece. Scoop the pâté into a container and transfer to the fridge for an hour to set. This can be done a day or two in advance.

4. Make the pastry shells. Roll out half of the puff pastry to 5mm (¼in) thick, and cut out six 12cm (4½in) discs. Place them on a couple of lined baking sheets. Beat the eggs, ensuring there are no streaks of yolk or white left in the bowl, and paint the top of each disc with the egg wash.

5. Roll out the other half of the pastry, again to 5mm (¼in) thick, and cut six more 12cm (4½in) discs. Make a cut inside them with an 8cm (3¼in) cutter, and discard the inside circle (or save to turn into cheese twists). Place the hollow circle on top of the painted 12cm (4½in) discs, so that it forms a border. You're essentially making large vol-au-vent cases: six rimmed pies. Paint the circles in egg wash, ensuring not to drip too much down the sides or they'll struggle to rise. Place a sheet of greaseproof paper over the top, to encourage the pastry to rise evenly.

6. Preheat the oven to 210°C/415°C/Gas 6–7. Bake the pastry for 15–20 minutes until risen and golden brown. Set aside.

7. To prepare the leeks, peel them of their outermost layers, and give them a good rinse under cold water. Cut into 2cm (¾in) slices, and place into the base of a large saucepan in a single layer, cut sides facing up. Pour the stock over the top and add the thyme, olive oil and a generous pinch of salt. Simmer incredibly gently (you don't want the leeks to fall apart, so they need to be barely moving) for 15 minutes.

8. Meanwhile, make the sauce. Rehydrate the porcini mushrooms in 5 tablespoons boiling water. Melt the butter in a small saucepan and add the sliced shallots. Fry for a couple of minutes, then add the garlic and cook until fragrant. Dice the rehydrated porcini and add to the pan, along with the chestnut mushrooms. Cook until golden brown. Sprinkle the flour into the pan, then stir. Pour in the alcohol and simmer away for a couple of minutes. Add the stock and cook until thick. Season with plenty of pepper and turn off the heat.

9. To prepare the chicken, set the oven at 200°C/400°F/Gas 6 and warm the butter in a large ovenproof frying pan. Fry the chicken skin-side down until crisp and golden, then transfer the pan to the oven for 15 minutes until cooked through. Leave to rest for at least 5 minutes before assembling.

10. While the chicken cooks, bring everything together – the pâté from the fridge, the leeks from the saucepan, the pastry from the baking sheet. Warm the sauce through to a very gentle simmer and add the cream.

11. Place the pastry shells on individual plates, push the pastry in the middle down so you have a well, and spread a generous tablespoon of pâté onto the base. Add a couple of rounds of leek, then slice each chicken thigh and add to the top. Bring the hot sauce to the table, and allow people to add their own.

I ended my birthday meal the way the characters do in the film: with a big wine-soaked, yeasted cake, surrounded by roasted fruit. It was delicious, but the honest truth is that by that point we were all so full that everyone could only handle a tiny piece. Here, then, I have stayed true to the lighter dessert of the book: a bottle of Sauternes arrives on the table, along with the canonical fruit – an assemblage of some of my favourites: peaches, figs and grapes.

It's impossible not to nod here to Diana Henry's glorious *How to Eat a Peach*, and the titular recipe within it. I've been dropping fruit into wine on a regular basis since my first reading.

GRAPES, FIGS, PEACHES AND SAUTERNES

Serves 6

3 peaches, pitted and cut into quarters
5 figs, stems removed, cut into quarters
100g (⅔ cup) black seedless grapes, halved
100g (½ cup) caster (superfine) sugar

CREAM
100ml (scant ½ cup) Sauternes
3tbsp caster (superfine) sugar
Zest of 1 lemon
200ml (scant 1 cup) double (heavy) cream

1. Put the peaches, figs and grapes in a bowl, tip the sugar over the top and toss it through. Cover the bowl and leave to macerate for an hour, or place in the fridge for up to 6 hours, if that makes your planning easier.

2. In a second bowl, pour the wine over the sugar and stir to help it dissolve. Add the lemon zest, then set aside until you're ready to serve.

3. To serve, add the cream to the wine and sugar and whip to very soft peaks. Divide the fruit between some nice glasses, and put a generous spoonful of the cream over the top.

Everything sounded like the Thanksgiving she wanted, which made the evening even more eerie. The guests looked festive and warm under the glow of the chandelier. The snow swirled effortlessly behind the front window panes. And the front hall of her home had switched to a dining room quite easily; it smelled like a mix of berries, brown sugar, baked crusts, and burning flames.

Such a Fun Age, Kiley Reid

It is a truth universally acknowledged that if a character spends a chapter roasting a turkey, making cranberry sauce and baking pumpkins into pies (or hiring someone to do the work for them), things are about to take a turn. It's a deeply satisfying inevitability: bringing characters together around a table will reveal their own holiday agenda and complicated histories. The quintessence of this is Kiley Reid's *Such a Fun Age*, where Thanksgiving arrives right at the point in the narrative where things need to be shaken up and reassembled. I don't want to spoil what happens for you (it is far too satisfying) but suffice it to say that Alix's perfect Thanksgiving dinner – both aesthetically and olfactorily exactly what she'd hoped – is derailed. Of course it is.

The visceral thrill of watching dinner falling apart, of things descending into chaos, lies in just how plausible it is. Even if our own families aren't running that risk, it's not too hard to imagine why one would. A trail of fuel is laid around grievances ignored or buried for years, secrets simmering beneath the surface, waiting for a spark to ignite it and set everything off.

It's less deliciously entertaining, of course, when it's your dinner party. That's the thing that's stressful about these big-ticket holiday dinners, the ones that come with the weight of history and tradition and expectation. Things can sound and smell and feel like the holiday you dream of – the spices, the fruit, the bird. But it's possible, too, that there's tension, that things are strange, that you're missing people who were there the year before, that there's a part of yourself you have to pack away in order to take a seat at the table. Perhaps there are questions you don't want to answer that you know will be asked, wounds that still ache when they are poked and prodded at, truces between family members that are tenuous and shaky.

I am extraordinarily lucky with my chosen family and friends, the people with whom I share my holiday table. We've always got along well; we love lots of the same food and films and games. We are all happy to facilitate each other's favourite traditions, as well as thumbing our noses at the ones we find too laborious or emotional or tricky. I have written a book about the joys and challenges of holidays (*The Little Library Christmas*) and don't wish to spend pages retreading old ground here. But I do think that it's the weight of expectation that makes things challenging, that makes a holiday meal carry something that a regular dinner with the family doesn't.

I have no easy fixes for this. Except to say, I suppose, that you owe nobody your holiday celebrations. If the family you were born into isn't the one you wish to spend a holiday with, if the idea of returning 'home' feels like anything but, it's worth considering what it might look like not to. Perhaps there is another family you've built who you can meet around the table with, perhaps you would rather go for a walk and have toasted sandwiches and read a good book and avoid the thing altogether. It's easier said than done, of course. Families are complicated, and traditions are too. But as the one who is more often than not in the kitchen, in charge of those sensory memories, I have taken to abandoning the traditions in tricky years. As soon as the turkey is off the table (so to speak) the weight of expectation eases somewhat. The day can be, suddenly, a little less tense, less likely to set everything alight, the temperature lowered to a gentle simmer. If only it had worked for *Such a Fun Age*'s Alix.

I turned to my friend Fiona for Thanksgiving advice when looking for something that smelled of the brown sugar and baked crusts from *Such a Fun Age*. I've been catering Thanksgiving dinners professionally for years now – I have my turkey, sides and pies routine down pat – but I wanted to talk to an American whose Thanksgiving food I once ate, and still regularly think about.

Her favourite pie is a pumpkin one, and though I have always made mine with shortcrust, she recommended a gingernut biscuit crust. I was immediately hooked; the spice and sweetness of the biscuits amplifies the filling. If you want to go the whole hog you can make this from roasted and puréed squash (most of the pumpkins we get in the UK are too wet to do the job), but it's getting easier and easier to find tinned pumpkin in supermarkets too. If you go this route, it's a gratifyingly simple pudding; if you're hosting Thanksgiving and already weighed down by tasks, this is the work of 30 minutes the day before.

PUMPKIN PIE

Serves 8

CRUST
250g (9oz) gingernuts (gingersnaps)
A pinch of salt
125g (4½oz) butter

FILLING
125ml (½ cup) double (heavy) cream
2tbsp cornflour (cornstarch)
1tsp ground cinnamon

A pinch of ground cloves
½tsp ground nutmeg
A pinch of ground black pepper
½tsp ground ginger
1x425g (15oz) tin pumpkin purée
2 eggs

TO SERVE
Whipped cream or crème fraîche

1. Blitz the gingernuts to fine rubble in a food processor, or tip them into a freezer bag and bash them by hand with a rolling pin. Add the salt, then melt the butter and pour it over the biscuits.

2. Press the buttery biscuits into a 20cm (8in) loose-bottomed tart dish, packing them along the base and up the sides. I find a drinking glass useful here for pressing them down and getting a really straight finish. Heat the oven to 160°C/315°F/Gas 2–3 and bake the base for 10 minutes; it will look damp and glistening when it comes out, because of the butter, but will solidify as it cools.

3. Pour the cream into a bowl, and whisk in the cornflour and spices. Add the pumpkin purée and the eggs and whisk to combine.

4. Pour the filling into the cooled base and turn the oven up to 180°C/350°F/Gas 4. Cook for 35–40 minutes, until only the centre of the pie is a little wobbly. Remove from the oven and leave to cool in the dish. Remove the pie from the pan, cover carefully (plastic wrap will stick to the set filling and destroy the smoothness of the top) and refrigerate for at least a couple of hours before serving. Serve with whipped cream or – my preference – crème fraîche.

In Katherine Heiny's *Early Morning Riser*, Taco Tuesdays at Jimmy's are a weekly ritual. Jane and her partner Duncan are the instigators. Duncan's ex-wife often joins them, along with her new husband, and Jane's friend Frieda sometimes comes too. I love them all, this hotch-potch of deeply human characters. And I love their dinners.

Taco Tuesdays don't always accurately describe what's on the table; sometimes it is tacos, sometimes a beef Wellington. But it's these enchiladas that I most fancied. I know the ingredient list seems lengthy, but this looks far more complicated than it is. It's doable for a mid-week dinner, and great for feeding a small crowd.

BLACK BEAN ENCHILADAS

Serves 4–6

SALSA*
1 x 800g (1lb 12oz) tin of tomatillos
2 brown onions, halved
4 garlic cloves
2 jalapeños
25g (1oz) fresh coriander (cilantro)
1tbsp lime juice
Sea salt

FILLING
2 dried ancho chillies
2 red onions, peeled and sliced
2tbsp flavourless oil
3 (bell) peppers (red, yellow or orange – green is too bitter here), cored and cut into long strips
½ cauliflower, cut into small florets
2tsp ground cumin
1tbsp dried oregano (Mexican, if you can get it)

2tbsp chipotle paste
1 x 400g (14oz) tin black beans, drained and rinsed**

SAUCE
250g (9oz) passata (strained tomatoes)
2tbsp chipotle paste
A pinch of dried oregano (Mexican, if you can get it)

TO ASSEMBLE
1tbsp flavourless oil
12 small or 8 large soft flour tortillas
250g (9oz) Monterey Jack or Red Leicester cheese

TO SERVE
200g (scant 1 cup) sour cream
Fresh coriander (cilantro)

* You can absolutely use a 350g (12oz) jar instead of making your own.
**If you can't find black beans, use aduki beans or kidney beans.

1. First, make the salsa. Place a heavy-bottomed frying pan over a moderate heat. Place the tomatillos, onions (still in their skins), garlic cloves (in their skins), and whole jalapeños in the pan, and cook until charred on all sides – about 20 minutes. Cool to room temperature.

2. Pop the garlic cloves out of their skins and peel and trim the ends off the onions. Put all the charred ingredients into a blender or food processor along with the coriander leaves and blitz to a chunky salsa texture. Taste and season with lime and salt, then set aside.

3. For the filling, cover the ancho chillies in just-boiled water to rehydrate them. While they do, fry the onions in the oil over a medium heat. Once the onion has begun to soften, add the peppers and cook for 5 minutes, then add the cauliflower, cumin and oregano.

4. Take the chillies out of the water and add their soaking liquid to the pan. Remove the stems, slice the chillies finely, and add them to the pan, along with the chipotle paste. Finally, add the beans and stir them through. Cook the filling for a further 10 minutes; the cauliflower should still have some decent bite. Stir half the salsa through the filling. Taste, season, and set aside to cool.

5. Put the sauce ingredients into a saucepan and simmer to thicken. Taste for seasoning.

6. Preheat the oven to 180°C/350°F/Gas 4. To assemble, rub the base and sides of a large baking dish with the oil. Spoon some filling into the centre of a tortilla, tuck the ends over, then roll up. Place in the dish (folded edges down). Repeat with the rest of the tortillas and filling, lining the filled ones alongside each other until the dish is full.

7. Spoon the sauce over the top, then finish with the grated cheese. Cover, and transfer to the oven for 25 minutes. Remove the cover, then cook for a final 5 minutes. Serve with the sour cream, some fresh coriander, and the rest of the salsa.

Nora Ephron's *Heartburn* (and the Meryl Streep film) reads as much like a menu of things I want to eat as it does a novel. Buttery mashed potato, key lime pie, bread pudding, bacon hash, perfect vinaigrette – heartbroken food writer Rachel cooks for others, for lovers, but, primarily, for herself.

Some of the recipes detailed within the narrative work better than others. But one of her casually impressive dinner-party dishes has made its way into my general culinary rotation: linguine alla cecca. Described by Ephron/Rachel as 'so light and delicate that it's almost like eating a salad', it's my go-to for summer evenings when the thought of serving a hot meal makes me want to cry.

LINGUINE ALLA CECCA

Serves 6

1kg (2lb 4oz) ripe tomatoes*
Ice
100g (3½oz) basil, leaves picked
1 garlic clove, squashed with the side
   of a knife

3tbsp extra virgin olive oil
¼tsp chilli flakes
600g (1lb 5oz) dried linguine
Flaky sea salt and black pepper

*When I'm making this for one, I use lovely cherry tomatoes. But slipping the skins from a kilogram of cherry tomatoes is a bit too masochistic for a simple mid-week dinner. Plum tomatoes (really fresh ones) will work too.

1. Fill your pan with water, and put it on to boil. Half fill a bowl with iced water. Slice a cross in the base of each tomato.

2. Once the pan of water is boiling, drop the tomatoes into it and leave them to bob along for a minute. Scoop them out and plunge them into the bowl of cold water to cool. Bring the pan of water back to a rolling boil, and salt it generously.

3. Drain the tomatoes then peel their skins off. I know – it's a faff. But

it's the whole point here; you want the tender flesh of the tomato to soak up all the oil and flavour. Cut them open, scoop out the seeds and remove the core. Roughly chop them or pull them apart (once deseeded, cherry tomatoes can be left as they are), and add them back to the bowl. Add the basil leaves, garlic, olive oil, chilli and a generous pinch of salt and black pepper. Mix together with your hands and allow to sit. Add the pasta to the now boiling cooking water.

4. When the pasta is al dente, reserve a mug of the cooking water, then drain the pasta and add it to the bowl. Toss everything together, lubricating with a splash of the pasta water if necessary, and more olive oil if you like. Remove the garlic clove. Serve immediately.

There are endless great dinners enjoyed by Elizabeth Jane Howard's Cazalets in her five-book series: poached salmon, asparagus soup, Charlotte russe. There honestly isn't a meal that I don't long to join them for. But there is a freedom in the kitchen and around the table in *The Light Years*, the first book. It is set in 1938, before characters and ingredients are missing, before the weight of fear and uncertainty has crept in, before Mrs Cripps and her team below stairs have rationing to consider. And so it is this early dinner of roast chicken and runner beans that I have chosen to recreate here.

I tried to do something 'different' with my chicken, but the truth is that rubbing it with a truly staggering amount of butter, and then resting it after roasting are the only rules worth following. If you have time, do try a dry brine (I was inspired by Samin Nosrat's *Salt, Fat, Acid, Heat*) as it makes the meat even more succulent. But if you don't, do not worry. This is roast chicken. It is supposed to be easy.

I often serve this with just a loaf of bread to dip into the buttery pan. But if you want the full Cazalet experience, mash potatoes with plenty of butter and bring to the table with some bread sauce (I make Nigella's; the recipe's online). But more often than not, all I want is the chicken, the beans and a good sliced loaf.

ROAST CHICKEN AND RUNNER BEANS AMANDINE

Serves 6

CHICKEN
1.8kg (4lb) chicken
3tbsp flaky sea salt (optional), plus 1tbsp
80g (5½tbsp) butter

BEANS AMANDINE
400g (14oz) runner (green) beans
75g (generous ½ cup) whole almonds
1 shallot

3 garlic cloves
50g (3½tbsp) butter
1tbsp lemon juice
2tsp lemon zest
Salt

TO SERVE
Crusty bread

1. If you've planned this dinner in advance, a dry salt brine is a good way to ready your chicken. Rub a generous amount of salt (3tbsp of flaky salt, half that much if you're using fine sea salt) into the skin and inside the cavity, and leave it in the fridge for 12–48 hours. The salt will draw moisture out of the meat and skin, season it, and will then be reabsorbed. Leaving the bird uncovered during this time will also dry out the skin, encouraging it to crisp up in the oven. If you don't have time for this step, start your dinner from Step 2 below.

2. An hour (on a warm day) or two (on a cold day) before you want to cook your chicken, take it out of the fridge and let it come to room temperature. Heat your oven to 190°C/375°F/Gas 5. If there's any moisture left on your bird, dab it dry with paper towels. Place it breast-side up in a roasting dish, and cut the string from the legs so they can fall open (this allows the thighs to cook evenly before the breast dries out). Before you put the chicken in the oven, rub it with the softened butter until the whole bird is covered in a generous layer, and then sprinkle all over with the tablespoon of flaky salt.*

3. Put the chicken in the oven with the legs pointed towards the back (it's hotter there) and roast for 70–90 minutes, depending on the weight. If you have a thermometer, the thigh meat should reach 75°C (167°F) once cooked. If you don't, poke a skewer into the thickest part of the thigh, and bring the chicken out of the oven when the juices run clear rather than pink. Cover with loosely tented foil, and leave to rest for 15 minutes.

4. While the chicken is resting, prepare the amandine ingredients. Top and tail the beans and slice into 8cm (3¼in) lengths, chop the almonds into rough slivers, and slice the shallot and garlic. Bring a pot of salted water to the boil and drop the beans in. Cook for

*This seems like an obscene amount of butter, I know. 80g is not a typo.

4 minutes then plunge them into iced water or drain and run under cold water.

5. Put the butter and almonds in a frying pan and cook over a moderate heat until the butter is foaming and a light nutty brown. Add the shallots and garlic and cook for a further 2 minutes, then add the lemon juice and 1 tablespoon of water. Add the beans to the pan, stir for a minute until they are all well coated, then transfer to a serving plate. Top with lemon zest and a sprinkle of salt. Bring to the table along with the chicken in its roasting dish, and plenty of bread for mopping up the chicken-y butter. There's no polite way to do this, so get your hands in and enjoy.

Since reading *The Light Years* I have made countless versions of Mrs Cripps's plum tart – there's one that's still online on my blog, a deep frangipane in a buttery shortcrust with plums baked into it. But here, in a chapter about dinner parties, I wanted something simple, something free-form, something that doesn't demand a loose-bottomed tart pan or anything beyond a baking sheet. I've rolled this pastry out with a bottle of wine in the absence of a rolling pin; you truly don't need anything fancy. It's not a classic English plum tart – it's unlikely to be exactly the one that Mrs Cripps would have made. But it's frankly so delicious that I hope she'll forgive me.

I feel that Mrs Cripps would be happy for me to suggest some seasonal alternatives too, for when the plums are yet to ripen on the trees at Home Place. Try the tart with sliced apple, ground almonds and nutmeg in autumn; with batons of rhubarb, ground ginger and ground pistachios in spring; and with whole seedless red grapes, cinnamon and walnuts in winter.

PLUM TART

Serves 6–8

PASTRY
200g (1½ cups) plain (all-purpose) flour,
  plus extra for dusting
A pinch of salt
1tsp ground cardamom
1tbsp caster (superfine) sugar
120g (4½oz) cold butter, cubed
1–2tbsp iced water

FILLING
400g (14oz) plums
75g (generous ½ cup) hazelnuts
45g (¼ cup) caster (superfine) sugar
2tbsp melted butter
1tbsp granulated sugar

1. First, make the pastry; it will need half an hour to rest in the fridge while you pit the plums. Tip the flour, salt, cardamom and sugar into a bowl, and add the chunks of butter. You can blitz this in a food processor if you have one, or you can rub it with your fingertips,

until the butter is in very small but still visible flecks. Bring the pastry together by hand, adding the water as needed. Shape into a disc and transfer to the fridge to rest.

2. Cut the plums in half and pull out their stones. If you have small plums, this is a time-consuming and fiddly job, but it's a worthwhile one – biting into a stone in your tart is less than ideal. If the stones are particularly tricky to dislodge, I find cutting through the equator of the fruit, instead of the poles, gives you more purchase: twist the top half off, and then twist the stone free.

3. Blitz or bash the hazelnuts until finely ground. This will be the work of moments in a food processor or spice grinder, but if you don't have one, a rolling pin will do the trick (or just buy ground hazelnuts, if you can find them). Mix with the caster sugar.

4. Preheat the oven to 180°C/350°F/Gas 4. Roll the disc of pastry out on a floured baking sheet, until around 35cm (14in) in diameter. The pastry should be 3mm (⅛in) thick. Sprinkle with the hazelnut and sugar mixture, leaving a 3cm (1¼in) border clear. Top with the plums, skin-side up, in a single layer (small ones can overlap a little if you can't fit them in).

5. Fold the clean edges up and over the fruit all the way around the tart, to form a makeshift crust. You'll need to pleat in various places; just ensure there are no points around the tart where plum juice could flow out.

6. Brush the crust and fruit with the melted butter, and sprinkle the crust with granulated sugar. Bake for 50 minutes to an hour, until the crust is golden brown, and the plums have collapsed. Serve warm or at room temperature with crème fraîche or ice cream.

The larger, noisier contingent of guests assembled their food in the kitchen. Lionel waited his turn, watching as they pirouetted and collided. They touched the smalls of each other's backs and shoulders. Men and women. They hugged and kissed and pressed against each other. Looped arms and hooked thumbs into each other's pockets. They poured wine and spooned things onto each other's plates.

'Potluck' from *Filthy Animals*, Brandon Taylor

There was a party for my birthday, a dinner party, as soon as it was legal. Ella cooked. Tash washed up. Richard and Katya and Ben brought wine and gifts and stories. I sat in the centre of things, while people looked after me. There were six of us, of course; we'd all become adept at dividing ourselves into groups of six.

It took a while, longer than I had expected, for a dinner party indoors to feel tentatively alright. It had been so very long since any of this had been permissible, had been safe. We had been told not to be close, not to hug, not to laugh too loudly, that to be appropriately social was to be distanced from each other. In the early days, I often imagined the time when it would all be over. I imagined it would be like those pictures of the end of the war – dancing in the street, a kiss with a stranger, street parties that stretched to include all of us who had come through it. I relied on the idea of it, was sustained by it as three weeks became six, then twelve. But the months crept on, and the sense that there would be a day when it was definitively over receded from view. When I spent time with people again, I instead hovered and hesitated. There was no dancing, no kissing of strangers. My thumb was hooked into no one's pocket.

I had survived alone for so long and had forgotten how I had done things Before. When I read Brandon Taylor's *Filthy Animals* that summer, the moment Lionel stands by the potluck table hit with such desperate ferocity that I caught my breath. Though our circumstances are entirely different – his re-entry to the world is after an extended stay in hospital, he is a Black man in the American Midwest, his 'friends' deserve inverted commas around the word – I recognized so tangibly the feeling of being on the edge of interactions. I found myself haunted by flashes of my friends as we once were, living in each other's pockets. The ease with which we used to bump elbows and collide and take up space alongside each other, the time when I was lucky enough to do so without thinking about it.

On my birthday, we greeted each other on the stairs at a respectful, careful distance, eyebrows raised in question. Are we okay? Are we too close? Are you hugging? But as the evening progressed, the space between all of us began to shrink. I relearned how to map it out, how to traverse it, how to eliminate it. We ate roast chicken, passing it around the table, hands touching as we pulled meat from the bones and dipped bread into buttery juices. We spooned things onto each other's plates. We poured wine. We pirouetted and collided. There was cheese, from a shared board, and a blackened blistered little custard tart for each of us.

Later, in the centre of things, I sat cosy and petted and adored. I looked a little mussed, in the mirror later, as I took my make-up off before bed. Mussed in a way that suggested hands around waists and heads resting on shoulders and endless hugs. Ease and affection and closeness – these things so longed for and the feeling of which I'd nearly forgotten after so long living alone. I hadn't looked that way in more than a year. I'd forgotten quite how much it suits me.

TEA
PARTIES

And really it was a wonderful tea. There was a nice brown egg, lightly boiled, for each of them, and then sardines on toast, and then buttered toast, and then toast with honey, and then a sugar-topped cake. And when Lucy was tired of eating, the Faun began to talk.

The Lion, the Witch and the Wardrobe, C. S. Lewis

This tea at Mr Tumnus's might very well be my platonic ideal. It's so many things I love in one meal: a soft-boiled egg, tinned sardines, plenty of toast and butter, some honey, a little cake. A pot of tea too, of course. It's all cosy, so reassuring and comforting. So English, really, in a way that comforts not because it's what I ate as a child, but because Lucy Pevensie did. Lucy, and Shirley Hughes' Alfie and Annie Rose, and the girls at Mallory Towers, and Dahl's Danny and William. Children I grew up with, by fires and in dormitories, who introduced me to this sort of meal. The circumstances of this particular tea are somewhat less than ideal: Mr Tumnus is trying to lull Lucy into a sleep so he can turn her over to the White Witch. But setting that moral quandary aside, it's a dreamy little afternoon – the snow, the fire, the menu.

Tea, as a meal, is the gentlest sort of hosting I can imagine; I'm never quite so relaxed when entertaining as I am when I've invited people around for tea. There is rarely any last-minute work to be done. You might take a cake out of a box, you'll probably need to boil the kettle, at a pinch some bread might need to be toasted. But, really, the majority of things in this chapter are easy to prepare in advance, and are best served at room temperature.

Though of course there's no age limit on a tea party, there's a reason that not just the event timing but the sort of food works well for children. It is achievable, preparation-wise, in those precious hours once the kids are in bed. For bigger numbers you don't have to worry about what goes together, or manage multiple courses – just put all the food on a large table and let people drift towards what they most fancy. It's sweet and cosy and crowd pleasing, eminently easy to graze your way through. It's the sort of food I made often in my nannying years, for the kids to take into school, for birthdays, late at night in anticipation of friends that would visit the next day.

A tea party is about the drink, of course. But it's actually more suggestive of a time, an afternoon sustenance between lunch and dinner. Before I moved to the UK, the best version I could imagine featured a tiered set of plates filled with dainty delicacies and hand-painted china pots filled with loose-leaf brew. It can be this, of course. I've played the tourist in the dining room at the Savoy, and filled up on fancy sandwiches and cakes. But the truth of it is that in my life it has always been a little less polished. I'm much more likely to be offering a collection of little fancies – some from a packet, some from the oven – to my friends' kids (or to my friends). The only tea party guest prerequisites are that they are thrilled by sweetness and company and silly games and icing around their mouths.

There's no way to follow up these musings on Mr Tumnus, on afternoon tea, on toast, without a recipe for sardines on toast. You don't really need a recipe for this, of course you don't. Squashing a tin of sardines into well-buttered toast is delicious – you don't need to go beyond that unless you fancy it. But as an enthusiastic advocate of tinned fish on toast, I want to offer you a couple of other options. All recipes give two portions (one for Lucy, one for Mr Tumnus), but they scale up easily if you're serving for a whole party.

SARDINE BUTTER ON TOAST

Drain the sardines from a tin. Add to a bowl with **30g (1oz) softened butter** and mash well. Season with **a dash of hot sauce** (Tabasco is my favourite here) and **a splash of Worcestershire sauce**. Divide between two well-toasted pieces of bread.

SARDINES, MINT, PEPPER AND VINEGAR ON TOAST

This is one for the best sardines – the fancy tins I pick up whenever I see them on offer or while on holiday. Lift the sardines out of two tins. Pour some **good olive oil** onto your toast and then lay the whole sardines on top (I am generous here – plenty of fat little fillets all snuggled up alongside each other). Dress with **a splash of white wine vinegar**, some **chopped fresh mint** and **white pepper**.

SARDINES AND AN EGG ON TOAST

Lower **two eggs** into simmering water, and cook for 6 minutes. Drain, run under cold water, peel, and cut each in half. **Butter** two slices of toast and squash half a tin of sardines onto each piece. Season with **black pepper** and sprinkle with **chopped fresh tarragon or dill**. Place two egg halves on each slice of toast, and season with **a sprinkle of salt**.

SARDINES AND CUCUMBER ON TOAST

Slice **half a cucumber** into ribbons using a vegetable peeler, stopping before you hit the seeds. Lay the ribbons on a piece of paper towel and sprinkle with **cider vinegar, fine sea salt** and **black pepper**. Leave for at least 10 minutes. Meanwhile, mash the fillets from a tin of sardines with **2tbsp cream cheese** and season with **a splash of vinegar**. Spread a generous layer of cream cheese onto each slice of toast, then add some ribboned cucumber. Spoon the sardine mix over the top and finish with another layer of cucumber.

I can picture these buns instantly: dark brown and rounded at their tops, sitting in their little white cases, crowded together on a plate. A tiger arrives and eats his way through the entire batch – not just one, but 'all the buns on the dish'. Judith Kerr's picture book is a classic for a reason, one of the best-known and most beautifully visually rendered tea parties in fiction.

Because I dearly love spiced buns, but I most particularly love the soft squidgy bits that are exposed when you pull the buns apart, I have gone slightly off-piste and decided not to put them in their little white cases.

SPICED BUNS

Makes 12

200ml (scant 1 cup) milk
50g (3½tbsp) treacle (molasses)
2tsp ground cinnamon
½tsp ground allspice
½tsp ground nutmeg
½tsp ground cardamom
A pinch of ground black pepper
A pinch of salt
100ml (scant ½ cup) double (heavy) cream
2 eggs
375g (2⅔ cups) strong white bread flour

100g (¾ cup) wholemeal (wholewheat) flour
7g (1½tsp) fast-action yeast
200g (1⅓ cups) sultanas (golden raisins)
Flavourless oil, for greasing
Butter, to serve

GLAZE
20g (1tbsp) treacle (molasses)
1tsp ground cinnamon
½tsp ground allspice
40ml (2½tbsp) boiling water

1. Warm the milk, treacle, spices and salt in a small saucepan over a low heat. Stir until the treacle is melted, bring it up to just below simmering, and then set aside to infuse and cool for at least 10 minutes. Stir the cream into the spiced milk and then whisk the eggs in too.

2. In a mixing bowl, or the bowl of a mixer if you'd rather use a dough hook than your hands for kneading, combine the flours and the yeast. Pour the milky-eggy mix in and combine to form a wet dough. Leave

for 15 minutes, until you can see tiny bubbles start to form. Add the sultanas.

3. Knead the dough, either by hand (10 minutes) or machine (5 minutes), until smooth. Cover the bowl and leave in a warm, draught-free place for an hour to increase in size by half.

4. Rub a little flavourless oil onto your work surface to prevent the dough from sticking, then scoop the dough out of the bowl. Divide into 12 even balls – sometimes I weigh them, and sometimes I play it by eye. Stretch the dough underneath itself so that it has a tight skin, then roll each ball under your hand until smooth and taut. Place on a lined baking sheet, leaving 1cm/½in between each ball – you want them to push up against each other as they rise. Leave them for at least an hour under a cloth (it could be 90 minutes or more in a wintry kitchen); they'll double in size and will bounce back when prodded once they're ready.

5. Preheat your oven to 200°C/400°F/Gas 6 and bake the buns for 22–25 minutes until risen and nicely browned. As they reach the end of their bake, add the treacle and spices for the glaze to a mug, and pour the boiling water over. Mix well, then paint the glaze over the hot buns once they come out of the oven. Eat warm, spread with a truly fantastic amount of butter.

The tea party that most satisfied my appetite as a child was Marmaduke Scarlet's feast in *The Little White Horse*. At the end of the action, when things have been mostly resolved, the inhabitants of Moonacre invite twenty or so guests over for afternoon tea. Marmaduke Scarlet, who has never knowingly under-catered, prepares more than twenty different dishes: cream horns, lemon-curd sandwiches, Cornish pasties, meringues, cinnamon toast. It's a culinary tour of English afternoon tea pleasures.

I didn't grow up on parkin; it was one of the (many) dishes in the novel I needed my mum to explain before I could picture it. A sticky, dark, spiced cake that's forgiving and easy to bake and should be slathered in butter? I was sold. Depending on my designs for the cake, I'll bake it either in my square pan, cutting it into generous squidgy bits for distributing on a stroll, or in a loaf for putting on the afternoon tea table. I've included timings for both below.

CORIANDER SEED AND ORANGE PARKIN

Makes 12-16 slices or squares

120g (½ cup) treacle (molasses)
120g (½ cup) golden syrup
120g (½ cup + 2tbsp) dark brown sugar
150g (⅔ cup) butter, plus 2tbsp to finish, and more to serve
60ml (¼ cup) milk
2 eggs
1tbsp coriander seeds (or 1tsp ground coriander)
200g (1½ cups) wholemeal (wholewheat) flour
150g (1 cup) medium oatmeal*
2tsp baking powder
2tsp ground ginger
A pinch of salt
Zest and juice of 1 orange

*Oatmeal is rubbly and coarse, a different product to porridge (rolled oats). It's in the cereal aisle in my supermarket, rather than with the baking ingredients.

1. Melt the treacle, golden syrup, sugar and butter over a gentle heat, and set aside to cool until you can touch the side of the saucepan. Whisk in the milk and the eggs.

2. Preheat your oven to 160°C/315°F/Gas 2–3. Roughly grind the coriander seeds, if using seeds, in a pestle and mortar. Combine the flour, oatmeal, baking powder, ginger and salt in a bowl. Pour the wet ingredients in, and stir everything together until you have a runny, deep brown batter. Finally, stir through the orange zest and juice.

3. Scrape the batter from the bowl into a lined pan – either a 25cm (10in) square one, or a 900g (2lb) loaf pan if you prefer. Bake the square pan for 50 minutes or the loaf pan for an hour, until the parkin is risen and springing back when prodded gently. Remove from the oven and paint with the final 2tbsp butter (if the butter is softened, the cake will be warm enough to melt the butter, so just rub it over the top with the back of a spoon).

4. Cool in the pan for 10 minutes, then turn out onto a wire rack to cool completely. Serve in generous squares or slices, spread thickly with butter. This cake will keep well for at least a week, and will be even better on the second and third days.

Half past four at Manderley brought a daily tea that haunts the second Mrs de Winter long after she finally escapes the house (and the presence of Mrs Danvers). There are crumpets, dripping with butter, a light angel cake, a denser fruit cake, little triangle sandwiches, and 'piping-hot, floury' scones. Though she'll probably never eat a scone again without some unsettling fear running through her, I have no such concerns. I bake them often, not least because a mere half-hour will take you from ingredients to afternoon tea.

There's a difference between a scone that has sat in a bakery window all day, and one that is pulled fresh from the oven. At room temperature, scones are robust, hearty, good for spreading thickly with butter. Still steaming inside, they're delicate, flaky and light. Du Maurier is specific here, and so I think we should follow her lead – leave your baking until the last possible moment for a Manderley-inspired batch of scones.

SCONES

Makes 12

280ml (1¼ cups) buttermilk – or yoghurt
  with 1tbsp lemon juice added
25g (2tbsp) caster (superfine) sugar
400g (3 cups) plain (all-purpose) flour,
  plus extra for dusting

4tsp baking powder
½tsp bicarbonate of soda (baking soda)
50g (3½tbsp) cold butter
1 egg

1. Preheat the oven to 220°C/425°F/Gas 7. Line a roasting pan with greaseproof paper and set aside.

2. Mix the buttermilk and sugar together in a bowl until the sugar is dissolved. Sift the flour, baking powder and bicarbonate of soda into a separate mixing bowl, then rub in the butter with your fingertips.

3. Add the buttermilk mixture to the dry ingredients, using a metal knife to stir to avoid overmixing. As soon as the mixture has come together into a dough, tip it onto a floured surface and sprinkle with a little more flour. Push down lightly with a rolling pin until the mixture is around 4cm (1½in) high. Dip a 6cm (2½in) round cutter in flour and push it down firmly, without twisting. Cut as many as you can from the dough and then reshape it with as little kneading as possible. Continue cutting out scones until all the dough is used.

4. Place the scones on a baking sheet, leaving at least 2cm (¾in) between each one for them to spread (though most of their rise will be upwards). Beat the egg and brush onto each scone with a pastry brush.

5. Bake for 12–15 minutes, removing the baking sheet from the oven when the scones are risen and golden on top. Eat immediately, split in half and spread with butter or clotted cream and your favourite jam. Put it on in whichever order you like – I refuse to be drawn into culinary battles fought across county lines.*

Rebecca is set in Cornwall, so I suppose technically you should put your jam on first. But let's face it, I've already thumbed my nose at authenticity by calling for buttermilk, so you can eat them any way you like.

In Elizabeth Gaskell's *North and South*, Margaret Hale and John Thornton first meet in Thornton's mill, a moment that allows for misunderstandings and snap judgements. Their second meeting is in a drawing room over tea and cocoa-nut cakes, laid out on a white tablecloth; in another book, it would be a scene ripe for flirtation. But by then it's already too late. Those opinions, so quickly formed, linger until the novel's final chapters.

We've all moved on from the era of the over-iced cupcake, I know, but they're still so easy to serve at a party – so neat, so pretty and so simple to distribute. These are based on Eliza Acton's coconut-gingerbread cake; perhaps fancier than those the Hale's cook Dixon would have made, but they need to 'flourish' alongside 'a basket piled high with oranges and ruddy American apples'. Just the thing you'd want to offer at a tea party with the strangely magnetic man who runs the local mill.

COCOA-NUT CAKES

Makes 12

CAKES
225g (1 cup + 2tbsp) dark brown sugar
Zest of 1 lemon
120g (4¼oz) butter
3 eggs
210g (1½ cups) plain (all-purpose) flour
1½tsp baking powder
120g (1½ cups) desiccated (dried shredded) coconut

2tsp ground cardamom

ICING
100g (3½oz) butter
2tbsp lemon juice
500g (3½) cups icing (confectioners') sugar
2tbsp milk
100g (2 cups) coconut flakes

1. Preheat the oven to 160°C/315°F/Gas 2–3. To make the cakes, tip the sugar into a mixing bowl and stir the lemon zest through. Beat the butter into the sugar until well combined; the mixture won't become pale or light as you'd expect with caster sugar.

2. Add the eggs, one at a time, beating after each addition. If the batter starts to separate, mix in a tablespoon of the flour to bring everything back together. Fold in the flour, baking powder, coconut, and cardamom. The batter will be thick – more like a biscuit dough than a pourable cake batter.

3. Divide between a lined or well-greased cupcake pan and bake for 20–23 minutes, until a skewer inserted in one of the cakes comes out clean. Cool in the pan for 10 minutes, then turn out onto a wire rack to cool completely (icing should never go on warm cakes).

4. To make the icing, beat the butter and lemon juice together, then add the icing sugar, a bit at a time, until them mixture is light and creamy. Beat the milk in too.

5. Drop a generous spoonful of icing onto the top of each cake. Wet a palette knife or flat butter knife and smooth the icing over the top. Finish with coconut flakes and serve.

Predominantly, we concerned ourselves with very happy memories, and those hours we spent together in the tea lounge were, I would say, extremely pleasant ones.

The Remains of the Day, Kazuo Ishiguro

Tea is, after water, the second most consumed drink in the world. Though in essence made by infusing the dried leaves of the *Camellia sinensis* shrub in water, tea is then prepared and served in many varied ways. In Japanese tea ceremonies, matcha (from green shade-grown leaves) is whisked into boiling water using a bamboo *chasen*. In India, chai is drunk with milk and sugar, the leaves boiled in with the water before the milk, sugar and spices are added to the still-simmering mixture. Tea in Turkey is served in small glasses throughout the day; despite these microdoses the country regularly tops the list in 'per capita' consumption.

Though tea has been drunk for nearly five millennia, we have only been drinking it in the UK since the mid-seventeenth century, when the British East India Company began importing goods from outside of Europe. There's not room here for us to delve into the violent colonial history of the tea trade; wars have been waged over it, trade deals struck over it, anti-slavery laws skirted to ensure continued production of it.* As all this was happening, consumption increased through the eighteenth century, when 'tea' became not just a drink, but a meal – high tea, afternoon tea, or plain old tea. It is now an inextricable part of the national culture, so much so that it's become

*If you're interested, as all those of us who drink tea should be, I recommend Lizzie Collingham's *The Hungry Empire: How Britain's Quest for Food Shaped the Modern World*.

shorthand for an invitation. I love it when people drop round for tea. I love the ease of the occasion, the way that it allows you to be impromptu, the fact that it can mean so many different things. A mug each standing up in the kitchen, a shared pot to linger over, cups set alongside a plate of biscuits or cake.

We drink some 63 billion cups of tea on this island per year, a number which seems at once extraordinary and – once I tally up my own daily intake – underplayed. It's hardly surprising. Tea is the correct answer in every emotional state, in every situation. Upon waking, when too cold (or too hot), when comforting a heartbroken friend, while flirting with someone you've brought home, after a funeral, to combat anxiety, to celebrate good news. Putting the kettle on is never inappropriate.

It appears constantly in literature too. Tea is the first occasion that brings Mr Bingley to the Bennet's in *Pride and Prejudice*, and tea is what Sir John and Mrs Jennings so frequently invite *Sense and Sensibility*'s Dashwoods over for. In Ishiguro's *The Remains of the Day*, it is tea that Stevens is preparing when Mrs Kenton announces her plans to be wed, and it is in the tea room of a seaside hotel that they meet for the final time. It is always teatime for the Mad Hatter and the March Hare in Wonderland as they rotate around a far-too-extensive number of chairs for their small party. Cecily and Gwendolen snipe over a pot of it when they first meet in *The Importance of Being Earnest*. There is so much tea drunk in *A Suitable Boy* that I quickly lost track of the cups. A cup of tea is what Arthur Dent most desires in *The Hitchhiker's Guide to the Galaxy* after Earth is destroyed for the sake of a new hyperspace bypass. It conveys so many things: hospitality, welcome, comfort, ritual, routine. It is so deeply everyday as to be nearly inconsequential. Except that, in literature at least, very little ever is.

The food in *Jane Eyre* is memorably awful. The writer Daniel Ortberg, on the now retired website The Toast, wrote an article ranking all the meals in *Jane Eyre* 'in Order of Severity'. He's not wrong – culinarily, it's a nightmare. But early in the narrative, Mrs Harden invites Jane and poor Helen (the descriptor indivisible from the character, at least in my head) to share in tea and toast. When there is only a morsel of toast available, she unwraps a 'good-sized' seed-cake, and they feast on it as if on nectar and ambrosia. This could be due to hunger, but I like to imagine it was the booze – this is a version of Mrs Beeton's 'very good' brandy-laced seed cake.

SEED CAKE

Serves 8

225g (1 cup) butter, plus extra for greasing
170g (¾ cup + 1½tbsp) caster (superfine) sugar
3 eggs
60ml (¼ cup) brandy

½tsp grated nutmeg
½tsp ground mace
225g (1¾ cups) plain (all-purpose) flour
1tsp baking powder
1tbsp caraway seeds
1tbsp demerara (turbinado) sugar

1. Make sure your ingredients are all at room temperature. Line the base of a 20cm (8in) baking pan with butter and greaseproof paper and preheat the oven to 160°C/315°F/Gas 2–3.

2. Beat the butter and sugar until light and creamy. In another bowl, whisk the eggs with the brandy, nutmeg and mace, then beat into the butter and sugar.

3. Sift the flour and baking powder into the mixture, and gently fold in along with the caraway seeds. Spoon carefully into the pan, flatten the top with a spatula and sprinkle with demerara sugar.

4. Bake for 50 minutes, or until a skewer inserted into the centre comes out clean. Cool on a wire rack, and serve in generous slices.

There's a walk I do often, from the centre of Stroud where I live, over to Slad, a village most famous for its literary resident Laurie Lee. Lee's memoir *Cider with Rosie* is so effective at transporting us there – to the icy family home, the fields covered in cowslips, the old schoolroom. Though the book is struck through with darkness, a picture of the sheer brutality of village life, it is a slice too of English nostalgia: blackberry picking, daytrips, festivals and parades. The schoolroom is transformed 'from a prison into a banqueting hall' for a party at one point, tables laid with brown buns, ham sandwiches, and fly-cake.

The fly-cake singular suggests this was probably a big fruit slice, cut into squares – not unlike the squashed-fly biscuits my great-grandmother used to store in a jar on her shelf. But it's not those I long for – it's fly-cakes, or Eccles cakes, one of my very favourite teatime treats. I drop in to buy a little white bag of them whenever I'm passing St. John Bread & Wine in Spitalfields. Traditionally, they're made with a lard pastry, but St. John's use puff pastry. Your own flaky pastry will be delicious, but the shop-bought version is great too, and makes these an even more achievable afternoon project.

ECCLES CAKES

Makes 8

PASTRY
200g (1½ cups) plain (all-purpose) flour
70g (5tbsp) butter
70g (5tbsp) lard – or butter, if you prefer
2tbsp very cold water
OR 320g (11¼oz) all-butter puff pastry

FILLING
25g (1¾tbsp) butter
50g (4tbsp) dark brown sugar

100g (¾ cup) currants
Zest of 1 orange
1tsp ground allspice
1tsp grated nutmeg

TOPPING
1 egg white
2tbsp demerara (turbinado) sugar

1. To make the pastry, blitz the flour, butter and lard in a food processor until the mix resembles breadcrumbs. Keep the motor running and add the water, a teaspoon at a time, until the dough comes together. If you're working without a food processor, you can do all this by hand – rub the fat into the flour with your fingertips, then stir the water through with the blade of a knife. Wrap the pastry and chill for at least half an hour.

2. While the pastry chills, melt the butter and sugar for the filling in a small saucepan, then stir in the currants, orange zest, allspice and nutmeg. Leave to cool completely, either on the work surface or in the fridge.

3. Preheat your oven to 200°C/400°F/Gas 6. Roll the pastry out to 5mm/¼in thick, or unroll your shop-bought sheet. Cut eight 10cm (4in) rounds of pastry. Put a tablespoon of the filling in the middle of each, then press down the edges of the pastry discs until they're thinner than the centre. Pull the sides of the pastry up over the filling, then pinch together with your fingertips. Turn each Eccles cake over and press the base around a little on the work surface until it is smooth. Neaten up the top, ensuring no fruit is peaking through, then transfer to a lined baking sheet.

4. Whisk the egg white until slightly foamy, then paint it onto each Eccles cake with the pastry brush. Make three slashes (for the Holy Trinity) in the top of each cake with a serrated knife. Sprinkle the top of each with some demerara sugar.

5. Bake for 20 minutes until golden brown and flaky. Serve at room temperature, ideally with Lancashire cheese. Laurie Lee was from Gloucestershire, I know, but this fly-cake is an Eccles cake, let's not forget.

Alongside the fairy bread (p109), and the ubiquitous packet of gently melting Tim Tams, Anzac biscuits were a sweet staple on the tea-party table during my childhood. They're iconic enough to be included in Mem Fox's *Possum Magic* – a picture book about possums eating their way around Australia. I've been making these biscuits for longer than I can remember; they taste like home.

ANZAC BISCUITS

Makes 16

125g (½ cup + 1tbsp) butter
3tbsp golden syrup
150g (1 cup + 2tbsp) plain (all-purpose) flour
100g (1 cup) porridge (rolled) oats

80g (1 cup) desiccated (dried shredded) coconut
90g (scant ½ cup) dark brown sugar
60g (⅓ cup) caster (superfine) sugar
½tsp bicarbonate of soda (baking soda)

1. Preheat the oven to 180°C/350°F/Gas 4. Melt the butter and golden syrup over a low heat and stir to combine. Put the flour, oats, coconut and sugars into a bowl and mix.

2. Add the bicarbonate of soda and 1 tablespoon of water to the golden syrup and butter, and stir. Pour this liquid over the dry ingredients and mix with a wooden spoon. The mixture should come together in clumps.

3. Shape ping-pong ball-sized spheres of the mixture and place onto baking sheets lined with greaseproof paper. Flatten slightly with the back of the spoon. If the biscuits crack at the sides, don't worry, just squidge them back together again.

4. Bake in the oven for 10–12 minutes until golden brown. The biscuits will feel underbaked when you take them out, but will harden on cooling. Err on the side of slightly underdone, as an Anzac biscuit should be chewy.

He grinned mischievously and held out his hand, holding two Tim Tams.

'I was a fairy-bread hogger at parties,' he told me seriously, his eyes immediately changing. 'I used to put them in my pockets or hide them whenever I could, until one day I was exposed when my host handed me my parka and four slices of fairy bread fell out.'

Looking for Alibrandi, Melina Marchetta

I've never been a particularly fussy eater. I have pretty catholic tastes and am, if anything, excessively hyperbolic about various foods, quick to identify ones I 'love' or which are my 'favourites'. Perhaps you've already noticed it – we're halfway through this book now, so I've almost inevitably done it multiple times already. I am so enthusiastic about everything that I know it can't possibly ring true – in frustration, my friend Liv once challenged me to list three foods I genuinely didn't like (I got stuck after kidneys and sour sweets). Truly, though, there is just so much I love to eat. And so it is entirely unsurprising that my memories of food in childhood are wide reaching, and overwhelmingly affectionate.

I could spend time here telling you about the ravioli I always ordered for my birthday at our local Italian restaurant (where the waiters would bring fizzy water for my sister and me in wine glasses so we could feel fancy). I could talk to you of Banana Paddle Pops that would melt faster than we could eat them, worth the pain of running barefoot over the hot bitumen of the service station carpark in pursuit of the huge chest freezer. I could tell you about my mum's pea and ham soup, which we made with the ham bone after Christmas and then froze until the cold July winter, when we needed it the most. I could tell you about the distinctive smell of the cheesy toast at Sizzler, about the joy of a warm plate pressed to my chest as I perused the salad bar. I could wax lyrical about tropical fruit in summer, about sucking on mango seeds or biting into pink slices of watermelon over the sink because everything was just so ripe and delicious that it was the only reasonable way to catch the drips. But, actually, I want to talk to you about tea parties, and fairy bread.

If you didn't grow up in Australia, there's a good chance you have no idea what fairy bread is. But if you spent your childhood at the suburban birthday parties that *Looking for Alibrandi*'s John Barton and I did, the mere sight of the words will strike joy into you. It's almost inevitable that a plate piled high with triangles of white bread, generously buttered and covered in hundreds and thousands (rainbow sprinkles) sat alongside the Cheerios, sausage rolls, and lamington fingers on the table. Honestly, it's hard to convey just how good fairy bread is, how simple, how worthy of hogging. It is the utterly perfect sum of its parts: soft bread, butter acting as both a glue and a slightly salty contrast, and the pleasing crunch of hundreds and thousands, providing the tooth-aching sweetness. I hadn't eaten a slice since those memorable birthdays but, in the interests of research for this book, I committed myself to a re-tasting. It was good enough to make me want to dig out the pass-the-parcel, set up a game of musical chairs, and head out into the backyard for a round of Red Rover.

WEDDING
PARTIES

The engraved menu card indicated that it was Giant South Sea Scallop Consommé with Washington State Ginseng Vapors and Black Mushrooms, but Rachel wasn't sure what to do when the white-gloved waiter at her side lifted the shimmering dome off her plate.

Crazy Rich Asians, Kevin Kwan

If you have spent more than a couple of hours in my company, there is a good chance that I've told you the story of the first time I catered a wedding. It was, to put things mildly, a complete fiasco. I blithely proposed and agreed to a menu that now (with years of catering experience under my apron) I would laugh at. We were so green, my team, so green and so hardworking and so optimistic and so drastically out of our depth. The marquee was like a sauna, half of the local waiting staff I'd organized didn't arrive, and I'd significantly underestimated how long it would take to carve the meat from an 80-kilo pig. Somehow, we pulled it off – the food went out, the guests loved it, and we collapsed in a pile on the floor of the kitchen.

And despite all the panic, the overly-complicated menu, the list of things that went wrong, the food managed to provide a template for the wedding catering my dear friend Olivia Potts and I do now – crisp, colourful salads, slow-roasted meat or charred vegetables rubbed in spices, good bread and butter, abundant canapés, a cake flavoured with herbs and fruit. It's the sort of food we love, not especially fussy or fancy, equally at home at a wedding breakfast or a Sunday lunch with friends.

The menu in *Crazy Rich Asians*, all foams and consommés and silver service, is consumed over numerous pages and to the general befuddlement of wedding guest Rachel. She's visiting her boyfriend Nick's Singaporean family for the first time and it's the wedding that the entire country has been talking about – quite literally no expense has been spared. It sounds extraordinary, the sort of tasting menu you'd save up for to try on an extravagant trip. But Rachel's at a wedding. It's time for crowd-pleasing food, rather than a menu so fancy you need instructions for it.

As we've made more and more wedding breakfasts, we have honed what it is that works, what people remember about their wedding meals in the years to come. Our canapés are generously sized, for that all important post-ceremony pre-dinner fizzy wine soaking up. We put the food down the centre of the tables, encouraging guests to break the ice while passing around a plate of well-dressed carrots. There's as much love put into vegetables as there is a joint of meat, so that carnivores and vegans can feast alongside each other. We want our food to feel familiar and comforting, just as much as we want it to be delicious.

The dishes that follow in this chapter can all be scaled up, if you ever find yourself in the unlikely situation of catering a large wedding. There are canapés (and more on pp159–170), some salads, a couple of mains, and a dessert, all of which will work for a crowd. More likely, you're going to be putting a nice lunch or dinner on the table for your loved ones, a worthy celebration of a slightly more manageable size, and so I have given you instructions that will work in your own domestic kitchen rather than a swelteringly hot hired marquee.

Aisling is a favourite of my Dublin-based sister Anna, who pushed the first of Sarah Breen and Emer McLysaght's series on me. The heroine is a winningly hapless small-town Irish woman who upends her life in pursuit of an unknown future in Dublin. In the third novel, *Once, Twice, Three Times an Aisling,* she is tasked with catering a friend's wedding. There's 'pork belly to cube, apple garnishes to slice, the potatoes for croquettes to boil and mash, pastry to roll...' As I read, I'm right there in the kitchen with her.

This is an Aisling-inspired version of one of our most requested canapés. The thing to look for is a decent, thick piece of belly. The belly my butcher sells is beautiful, from our local Gloucester Old Spot pigs; regardless of where you're buying, the general rule here is that you want some meat with the fat.

PORK BELLY WITH PICKLED APPLE

Makes 20 canapés, enough for 4–6 alongside other nibbles

400g (14oz) slab of pork belly
500ml (generous 2 cups) Guinness – or a 440ml (16oz) can topped up with water
2 sprigs of rosemary
3tbsp treacle (molasses)
1tsp smoky paprika
1tsp flaky sea salt

PICKLED APPLE
1 very crisp eating apple
50ml (3½tbsp) cider vinegar
1tsp flaky sea salt
½tsp sugar

EQUIPMENT
Cocktail sticks

1. Preheat the oven to 150°C/300°F/Gas 2. Put the belly skin-side up in a roasting dish that doesn't leave the pork with too much wiggle room. Pour the Guinness in, then add the rosemary and treacle. Cover the dish with foil and transfer to the oven for 3–4 hours, until the meat is entirely tender. Test this by prodding at one side with a fork; the pork should pull away easily.

2. Remove from the oven, and allow the meat to cool a little. Pull

it out of the Guinness (be careful as it can fall apart), and wrap the whole slab very tightly in plastic wrap. Refrigerate for at least 6 hours, ideally overnight. Keep the cooking liquor in the fridge too.

3. Prepare the pickle at least an hour before serving; a jar of it will be okay for a good few hours, but any longer and it will become too mushy. Use a vegetable peeler to slice the apple into ribbons, skin and all. Bring the vinegar to a simmer with the salt and sugar, then pour over the ribbons. Cover and place in the fridge.

4. Once it has had its time in the fridge, unwrap the pork and carefully slice the skin off the top, leaving behind as much of the fat as possible. Preheat the oven to 220°C/425°F/Gas 7. Slice the pork into neat squares, and arrange closely side by side in a roasting dish with the fat that sat under the skin facing up.

5. Pour the reserved cooking liquor into a saucepan. Add the paprika and salt and bring to the boil. Reduce until glossy and a little sticky. Spoon a little liquor over the pork and transfer to the oven for 20 minutes. Remove from the oven, and turn the heat up to 240°C/475°F/ Gas 8. Spoon the rest of the liquor over the pork, and return to the oven for a final 5 minutes, until the fat is crisp and brown on top.

6. While the pork is cooking, roll the ribbons of apple and pierce through each piece with a cocktail stick.

7. Take the pork from the oven. Poke the cocktail sticks into the pork, so the apple sits on top. Serve hot, but wait for at least a couple of minutes; the fat and sugar will be molten straight out of the oven and the last thing you want is a blister-mouthed guest.

A note: If you want to eat this as a main, skip the overnight chill. After step 1, turn the heat up, remove the skin and continue cooking as in step 5. It's delicious piled into tortillas with lettuce and pickles, or on sticky rice with stir-fried greens.

Maggie Shipstead's *Seating Arrangements* is set on a New England island over the course of a weekend wedding. It's a comedy of manners (and of errors); a collection of mostly awful people who share an extraordinary, knotted, complicated amount of history.

Culinarily, the high point of the weekend is the first-night dinner, prepared over multiple chapters. The lobsters show up in crates, plenty of Champagne is poured, and trays of salmon and shrimp cocktail are passed around. Here is my canapé version of this classic.

PRAWN COCKTAIL CANAPÉS

Makes 20 canapés, enough for 4–6 alongside other nibbles

1 egg yolk	1tbsp sriracha
1tsp lemon juice	225g (8oz) small cooked prawns (shrimp)
1tsp Dijon mustard	¼ cucumber
150ml (scant ⅔ cup) light olive oil or rapeseed (canola) oil	2 little gem (Bibb) lettuces
2tbsp tomato ketchup	1tbsp finely chopped chives
	A pinch of cayenne pepper

1. For the sauce, whisk the egg yolk with the lemon juice and mustard in a small bowl. Whisk in the oil, a little at a time, until you have a thick mayonnaise. Add the ketchup and the sriracha, then taste – I like mine fiery. When you're happy, mix the prawns through the sauce, then cover and store in the fridge until you're ready to assemble.

2. Slice the cucumber into thin half-moons. Cut the base off the little gems, and wash the leaves in cold water. Pat dry with paper towels.

3. To assemble, cut the curled tips off the lettuce leaves. The pieces should be robust enough to carry the filling – the outermost leaves might be too soft. Shred the base of the leaves and any offcuts and stir though the prawns. Spoon a few prawns onto each leaf, and add the cucumber. Top with some chives, and a sprinkle of cayenne pepper.

Cold Comfort Farm's Flora Poste is one of literature's great party planners. Orphaned, and confident that there is no limit to 'the amount one may impose on one's relatives', she moves to Sussex to live on a farm with a distant branch of her family: the Starkadders. Our heroine is urban – brisk and sensible – and utterly despairs of her feckless relatives. She takes it upon herself to fix things: to build careers, challenge norms, and plan a wedding. It is young Elfine who is married, on Midsummer's Day, the ceremony followed by caviar, syllabub and crab patties for the Starkadders, and by cold-cured ham, bread, and 'salads made from local fruit' for the county.

When Liv and I are planning wedding menus, it is the salads I am always most excited by. Because we serve family style, platters of seasonal salads make up the bulk of our wedding breakfasts. The ingredients are pickled, roasted, toasted, blitzed and then tossed together in a way we hope makes them memorably delicious. Stella Gibbons was talking about fruit salads for pudding, I suppose, but here I'm proposing three very special savoury fruit salads.

COURGETTE, CHERRIES, LEMON, BURRATA

I'll eat burrata with just about anything, with grilled green vegetables, with ripe tomatoes, on its own and drowned in olive oil. It makes for a really special dish here; be sure to leave the cheese whole so your guests can cut into it at the table.

Serves 8 as a side, or 4 for lunch

4 medium courgettes (zucchini)
Juice and zest of 2 lemons
3tbsp olive oil
100g (3½oz) watercress, leaves picked

25g (1oz) parsley, leaves picked
200g (7oz) pitted cherries
2 large burrata
Flaky sea salt

1. Slice the courgettes into thin ribbons using a mandoline or vegetable peeler. Put the strips into a serving dish with the juice of

one of the lemons (you'll need the zest at the end, so be sure to zest them before juicing them) and a pinch of salt. Toss to coat, then leave for 10 minutes. Add the watercress and parsley then dress with most of the olive oil.

2. Squash the pitted cherries slightly, put them in a bowl with the juice of the other lemon and give them a good stir. Dot them across the top of the salad. Make a couple of indents in the salad, drain the burrata, and drop them in (carefully, so as not to split them). Sprinkle the lemon zest over the burrata, and add a final drizzle of olive oil and a pinch of flaky salt.

CUCUMBER, FENNEL, STRAWBERRY, DILL

This is bright, fresh and vibrant: a true summer joy. Although the ingredients here are ones I associate with English summers, as I ate it I realized it's not dissimilar to *okroshka* – a Russian spring herb and vegetable soup – with pickled strawberries replacing the sharp gherkins, and a yoghurt dressing stepping in for the kefir and kvass.

Serves 8 as a side

150g (5½oz) strawberries, hulled and cut
  into slices*
3tbsp cider vinegar
A large pinch of black pepper
1 fennel bulb
Juice of 1 lemon
200g (7oz) radishes
2 cucumbers
20g (¾oz) dill fronds, leaves picked

DRESSING
2 garlic cloves
A pinch of salt
200ml (scant 1 cup) yoghurt
2tbsp olive oil

TO FINISH
2tbsp cumin seeds

*Ideally, you should pick up slightly underripe strawberries if you can – the ones still white near their stems, rather than a completely vibrant lipstick red. If you can only find really ripe ones (you lucky thing) reduce the pickling time to 10 minutes, or you'll end up with strawberry mush.

1. First, get your strawberries pickling. Place the slices into a bowl and cover with the cider vinegar and black pepper. Leave for 20 minutes while you get on with prepping everything else.

2. Make the dressing. Mince the garlic cloves finely, add the salt (chop it through the garlic) and whisk through the yoghurt, then whisk in the olive oil. Set aside.

3. Toast the cumin seeds in a dry pan until they are lightly browned and fragrant. Set aside.

4. Finely slice the fennel with a mandoline, or as thinly as you possibly can with a knife, then place in a bowl and toss with the lemon juice. Cover with plastic wrap or a damp tea towel so that it can soften slightly in the acid of the lemon without going brown.

5. Top and tail the radishes and slice them finely. Slice the tops off the cucumbers and cut on the diagonal into thin slices.

6. Add the lion's share of the dill to the sliced vegetables. Toss all the vegetables together with the strawberries and the dressing and store in the fridge for up to an hour before serving. Serve on a flat plate, topped with the remaining dill and the cumin seeds.

PEACH, RICOTTA, TOMATOES, HERBS

There's a peach salad in Jamie Oliver's *The Naked Chef* that my sister Luce and I discovered when we were little, and used to make as often as we were allowed. It has peaches and basil and prosciutto and it felt like the fanciest salad I could imagine. There's a salad Diana Henry does too, with tomatoes and peaches and basil: a true summer dream. This salad has roots in both, with huge handfuls of herbs, creamy cool ricotta, and some pickled red onion.

When peaches are in season, it's sublime – fresh and fragrant and bright.

Serves 8

1 large red onion, finely sliced into
   half-moons
2tbsp sherry vinegar
800g (1lb 12oz) tomatoes
4 peaches

3tbsp olive oil
100g (3½oz) bunch of mint, leaves picked
100g (3½oz) bunch of basil, leaves picked
200g (7oz) soft ricotta
Salt and black pepper

1. First, get the onion pickling. Put the slices into a large bowl and pour the vinegar over. Add a small pinch of salt and squeeze the onion with your hands until it starts to soften, then leave to sit in the bowl.

2. Cut any cherry tomatoes in half, and then larger tomatoes into similarly sized chunks.

3. Be gentle as you're prepping the peaches – there's a reason why we talk about people bruising like them. Slice through the middle and gently twist, then pull the stone out. Cut into wedges.

4. Whisk the oil into the sherry vinegar and red onion, and season generously. Add the tomatoes, peaches and herbs, and gently toss together with your hands. Dot with spoonfuls of the ricotta and serve.

...the bustle in the house and all the preparations had excited me, and it seemed to me a festivity from beginning to end. The breakfast was such as best breakfasts then were: some variety of bread, hot rolls, buttered toast, tongue or ham and eggs. The addition of chocolate at one end of the table, and the wedding cake in the middle, marked the speciality of the day...

Reminiscences, Caroline Austen

It is very rare for a wedding breakfast to be an actual breakfast. Caroline Austen might recall the buttered toast at her sister's wedding, Vincent and Misty might feast with their friends on eggs, bacon, sausage and kippers in Laurie Colwin's *Happy All the Time*, but at the weddings I've attended, I've yet to see a toast rack on the table after the ceremony. It's a shame, really. I love toast (a note: please do invite me to your breakfast-y weddings – I am a delightful guest, will tell you endlessly and very sincerely how beautiful you both look, and will cry at all the appropriate moments).

Etymologically, the phrase wedding breakfast is a bit of a question mark. Its first recorded use is in Victorian England, but it seems possible that its roots are pre-Reformation. In the Middle Ages, before Western European nations began that mid-millennia reckoning with Catholicism, bridal couples fasted before taking communion during their ceremony; the meal that followed the service allowed them to break their overnight fast. A breakfast, then, but not in the toast and porridge way that the word now calls to mind.

Across the world, there are countless culinary traditions associated with weddings; from the food the couple break their fast with, to the edible favours guests take home with them. In Germany a *hochzeitssuppe* (a wedding soup) is served during the reception, a humble dish made from meat, noodles, herbs and vegetables. In Brazil, guests go home with *bem casados*, sandwiched biscuits filled with sweet dulce de leche. A tea ceremony often follows the marriage in China. At some West African weddings, kola nuts are either exchanged between families, or are blessed and then broken. The tradition of giving sugar-covered almonds, to represent the potential bitter and sweet of married life, originated in the Italian town of Sulmona. A South Indian custom at Hindu weddings is the *talambralu*, during which the couple shower each other with rice, saffron and turmeric. In Bulgaria, mothers of the bride and groom will feed the couple bread and honey, in hopes of ensuring a sweet life together.

I didn't grow up imagining a perfect dress, or a wedding colour palette, or even a dream menu. There were no shortage of weddings in my childhood, but the rituals that surrounded them seemed movable, rather than strict. I've watched friends and family marry in churches, in restaurants, in hotels, in fields, in registry offices. I've feasted on wheels of Parmesan that glistened with salt, on a croquembouche decorated with crystallized violets, on a slice of perfectly rare venison wellington, on platters of oysters, on a selection of snack bags from a crisp buffet. My dad was married in the Botanical Gardens, surrounded by late-summer flowers. My mum eloped in a black dress, on the beach, and we woke up the next morning to a breakfast barbecue. I have no idea what my wedding might look like. But I imagine, toast-lover that I am, that it will include breakfast.

The hours that follow Ursa's wedding in Kiran Millwood Hargrave's *The Mercies* are spent in the back room of a pub, 'a bottle of brandy between the men'. It is far from what she had dreamed – she wanted roasted goose, creamed spinach, buttery carrots, a salmon poached in lemon and chives, and candles that threw golden light around the room. There is so much darkness to come in the pages that follow that I found myself wanting to cook this for her. It's richer than the salmon Ursa is dreaming of, but I want salmon that's almost absurdly luxurious, the best you'll ever eat.

This salmon is roasted in such an extraordinary amount of butter that it gently poaches. It is elegant, and gorgeously tender, a truly show stopping dish for a wedding breakfast or celebratory feast. Serve this with some little boiled potatoes, and a sharp green salad. It's also lovely with the slaw from p30 or the courgette salad on p120 (the burrata may be too rich, so leave them out if pairing it with this salmon).

BUTTER POACHED SALMON WITH LEMON AND CHIVES

Serves 6–8

800–900g (1¾–2lb) side of salmon, skin
  on, descaled
75g (2¾oz) butter, softened
2 lemons
Sea salt

CHIVE OIL
Bunch of chives
100ml (scant 1 cup) light olive oil

1. First, make the chive oil. Blanch the chives by pouring a kettle filled with boiling water over them, and then refreshing under cold water. Pat dry with paper towels. Pack the chives into a food processor (you can also do this with a blender or stick blender), then add the olive oil. Blitz for a couple of minutes, until the oil turns a vivid green with no visible chunks of chive. Set aside for at least an hour to infuse, then

strain through a fine muslin (cheesecloth) or sieve. The strained oil will keep for a week in the fridge.

2. Preheat the oven to 140°C/275°F/Gas 1. Pat the salmon dry, and find a roasting dish that the whole piece can fit into. Line the dish with greaseproof paper and lay the salmon in skin-side down.

3. Prepare the butter. It should be soft enough to spread; if it's cold in your kitchen, soften it in the microwave or put it on a plate in the oven while it heats up (do keep an eye on it). Zest and juice one of the lemons, and add the zest and juice to the butter, mixing it through.

4. Spread the butter over the salmon in a thick layer. Season with a little salt – only a little, as your butter is salted – and then transfer to the oven. Cook for 20 minutes, until the salmon is just starting to flake.

5. Slice the other lemon into wedges. If you're transferring the fish to a serving plate then very gently lift the paper and slide the fish onto the plate. Alternatively, keep the fish in the roasting dish. Bring the whole fillet to the table, allowing people to serve themselves; the flesh will easily come away from the skin. Serve with the lemon wedges and a bowl of the chive oil.

The wedding that opens Mario Puzo's *The Godfather* sees hundreds of guests gathered in the garden, flowers everywhere, long tables laden with food and bottles of homemade wine. In the film, that food is lasagna – a Sicilian one, probably, given what we know of Don Corleone and his family. Hoping to make a version that would honour this wedding, I asked food writer Rachel Roddy, who's based in Rome but has written extensively about the food of Sicily too, for a steer on a Sicilian wedding lasagna. We talked about the line between baked pasta and lasagna (the latter isn't as common in Sicily as the former), considered the famous timpano from *The Leopard*, and landed on lasagna that screams 'event' – one where each new layer (meatballs! peas! ricotta!) only adds love and ceremony to the whole.

My friends Katya and Ben had lasagna at their wedding too, a great dish of it delivered to each table alongside big green salads and great bread. It was delicious, convivial, and achievable for the 400-something of us who sat at round tables in a Hackney chapel. A far more relaxed atmosphere than the undercurrent of tension running beneath Connie Corleone's nuptials, and a feast that set us up for the hours of dancing ahead.

A LASAGNA FOR A FEAST

Serves 8

RAGÙ
1tbsp olive oil, plus extra for greasing
100g (3½oz) minced (ground) pork
400g (14oz) minced (ground) beef
1 onion, finely diced
2 carrots, finely diced
2 celery sticks, finely diced
3 garlic cloves, minced
2tbsp tomato paste
200ml (scant 1 cup) marsala or red wine

1 x 400g (14oz) tin chopped tomatoes
150ml (scant ⅔ cup) milk
Flaky sea salt and black pepper

MEATBALLS
200g (7oz) minced (ground) pork
1tsp ground fennel seeds
1tsp sweet paprika
1tsp dried oregano
A large pinch of ground black pepper

A large pinch of flaky sea salt
2tbsp marsala

BÉCHAMEL
50g (3½tbsp) butter
50g (6tbsp) plain (all-purpose) flour
500ml (generous 2 cups) milk
2 bay leaves

Fresh nutmeg
White pepper

TO ASSEMBLE
8 hard-boiled eggs
200g (7oz) frozen peas
250g (9oz) dried lasagne sheets
250g (9oz) ricotta
125g (4½oz) Parmesan, finely grated

1. First, make the ragù. In a large saucepan, heat the oil and fry the pork and beef until browned. Scoop it out of the pan and set aside, leaving the fat behind. Fry the onion, carrots and celery until soft, then add the garlic and cook for a couple of minutes.

2. Add the meat back to the pan, and stir in the tomato paste and the marsala. Pour in the tin of tomatoes (swirl some water around the tin and empty it into the pan too). Add the milk and bring to the boil.

3. Turn the heat down, half cover with a lid (so you don't get tomato all over your worktop, but so that some of the liquid can evaporate off) and simmer gently for an hour while you prepare everything else. Once thick and rich, taste for seasoning and set aside.

4. To make the meatballs, season the pork with the ground fennel, paprika, oregano, black pepper, salt and marsala. Squidge together with your hands, then shape into 30 marble-sized balls. Fry the meatballs in a dry pan (there's enough fat in the pork to prevent them sticking) until browned outside.

5. To make the béchamel, melt the butter in a saucepan, tip in the flour and cook for a couple of minutes, stirring constantly. Add a splash of the milk and whisk in. Keep adding the milk in stages, whisking until smooth each time, then drop in the bay leaves. Cook at a very gentle simmer for 5–10 minutes until thick enough to coat the back of a spoon. Taste, season with nutmeg and white pepper and set aside.

6. Peel the eggs and slice them in half lengthways, and run the frozen peas under cold water.

7. Once all the component parts are ready, it's time to assemble the lasagna. Grease a large dish – mine is 35 x 25cm (14 x 10in) – and spoon a third of the ragù into the base. Top with half the béchamel, then dot the meatballs over the top. Cover with a layer of lasagne sheets. Spoon the next third of the ragù over the pasta, then scatter the peas over the top, and spoon the ricotta over the peas. Top with another layer of pasta, then add the rest of the ragù.

8. Press the eggs, yolk side up, into the ragù. Pour most of the béchamel over the eggs, setting aside about 100ml/scant ½ cup for the top. Add a final layer of pasta, the last of the béchamel, then the Parmesan. Cover the dish in foil, and set aside for an hour before it goes in the oven.

9. Preheat the oven to 200°C/400°F/Gas 6, and cook the lasagne for 30 minutes, then remove the foil and cook for a further 20 minutes until a deep, rich brown. Allow to rest for at least 15 minutes before cutting into it – your slices will be neater once you've given it a moment, and you don't want your guests' mouths scorched!

I've made a few versions of Baked Alaska, and they're all great; cake, ice cream and meringue are a winning combination. But this Baked Manhattan – a riff on the bourbon, sweet vermouth, orange bitter and cherry in the cocktail – is a very special one, made to honour Kay and Harald's New York nuptials in Mary McCarthy's *The Group*. When the Baked Alaska is brought out, the guests' joys are magnified – it's the dessert of 'childhood dreams come true'. It's a joy they hold onto even though the dessert itself is a bit underwhelming, unevenly browned with the cake below a bit stale.

That isn't the case here. This is a boozy, sharp, delicious, entirely grown-up pudding, ideal for a very *very* special occasion. It has multiple steps and component parts, and a little bit of last-minute high-stakes magic – either a brief flash in a hot oven, or a flourish with a blowtorch. It's a showstopper, in the truest sense of the word. People will gasp, I promise you.

BAKED MANHATTAN

Serves 6–8

ICE CREAM
80g (2¾oz) finely cut marmalade
500ml (17oz) good vanilla ice cream
Zest of 1 blood orange – if they're not in season, use a regular orange

CAKE
100g (3½oz) butter, plus extra for greasing
100g (3½oz) light brown sugar
2 eggs
50g (3½tbsp) yoghurt
2tbsp bourbon or rye whiskey
150g (1 cup + 2tbsp) plain (all-purpose) flour
2tsp baking powder

A pinch of salt

JAM
150g (5½oz) good cherry jam
2tbsp sweet vermouth

SYRUP
3tbsp caster (superfine) sugar
3tbsp bourbon or rye whiskey
Juice of the zestless orange from the ice cream

MERINGUE
4 egg whites
200g (1 cup) caster (superfine) sugar

Some notes on equipment:

• I'm afraid I am going to recommend you get hold of a blowtorch. You can, of course, put a Baked Alaska in a hot oven (for those nervous around a blowtorch, I have included directions below). But there is simply no way I'd do without one for a wedding; you want the ice cream from freezer to table as quickly as possible, and a blowtorch is the way to do that. Pedants will tell you a blowtorched 'Baked' Alaska is not a Baked Alaska; ignore those losers. They don't deserve you, or your dessert.

• As I'm already recommending you procure a blowtorch, I don't want to tell you that you also have to go out and buy a new cake pan and pudding basin. Use what you have, and trim your cake if necessary; the cake should have a diameter a good 3–5cm (1–2in) wider than that of the base of the ice cream, so you have a couple of centimetres leeway each side. I've gone with a common 20cm (8in) pan in the hopes that the timings will work with what you have. If not, keep a more committed eye on it during baking.

1. First, prepare your ice cream. You can make your own, if you like, but I'm going to recommend adding some flavour to a shop-bought tub; it has a great slicing consistency that will make serving a dream. Prepare a bowl to set it in – a 1-litre (1-quart) pudding basin is ideal as it's deep and not too wide – by lining it with greaseproof paper or plastic wrap. Warm the marmalade in a small saucepan. Scoop the ice cream from the tub into a mixing bowl and stir the softened marmalade and the orange zest through the scoops. Work quickly so it doesn't become soupy; it doesn't need to be evenly distributed – ribboned is fine. Press the flavoured ice cream firmly into your lined bowl, cover and freeze for at least 8 hours, or overnight.

2. For the cake, grease and line a 20cm (8in) cake pan, and preheat your oven to 160°C/315°F/Gas 2–3. Cream together the butter and sugar in a mixer or by hand, until smooth and no longer grainy with the sugar. Whisk together the eggs, yoghurt and whiskey, then beat into the butter and sugar. Fold in the flour, baking powder and salt.

3. Pour the batter into the lined pan and bake for 25–30 minutes, until the cake is risen and a skewer comes out clean. Allow to rest for 10 minutes in the pan, then turn out onto a wire rack to cool completely.

4. Spoon the jam into a small saucepan and add the sweet vermouth. Stir over a moderate heat until well combined and reduced a little, then set aside to cool.

5. To make the syrup, dissolve the sugar in the bourbon and orange juice over low heat, stirring until the liquid is thick and syrupy.

6. Slice the cake in half through the centre. Place the domed top of the cake upside down on a serving plate (one that can go in the oven if you're going to finish the meringue there). Paint half the syrup onto the cake, encouraging a generous amount of it to soak in.

7. Spoon the cooled jam onto the centre of the cake and spread it over, leaving a 1cm (½in) gap at the edge so that the jam doesn't find its way into the meringue. Place the other half of the cake on top, and soak with the rest of the syrup. Cover until you're ready to serve.

8. To make the meringue, place the egg whites and sugar in a heatproof bowl over a pan of simmering water. Whisk gently over the heat until the sugar is completely dissolved – rub a little between your fingers to check; you shouldn't feel any grains. Beat to firm peaks with an electric hand whisk or in a mixer, continuing until the meringue is cool. If you're going to finish the meringue in the oven, preheat the oven to 230°C/450°F/Gas 8.

9. To assemble, take the ice cream from the freezer, and invert it onto the centre of the cake. Pipe, spoon or smooth a layer of meringue over the ice cream and cake. I think palette-knife smoothed sides looks very chic, but I have great affection for peaked meringue too. Honestly, have fun with it.

10. Lastly, the meringue needs to be torched or baked. Fire up your blowtorch and expose your meringue to the fierce flame, or put the whole dessert in your hot oven for 4 minutes, until gently browned.

There are lots of love stories I considered when thinking about including a recipe for a wedding cake. Anne and Gilbert win out, in the end, because they get married in an orchard, in autumn, and because they're perfect. Their tempestuous beginnings, that early competitiveness, develops over the course of several books into a love story I was swoony about in my pre-teen years. And, to be clear, remain so about now.

Autumn is my favourite season when we're catering weddings. All the gorgeous late-summer produce is still available at the greengrocer, but the autumn vegetables, and the apples, have arrived. The light is golden and low in the sky, and the changing leaves provide a glorious backdrop. This cake is a true celebration of the season, and of the orchard: it's dark and spiced (as Anne and Gilbert's wedding cake probably would have been, given the history of fruit cakes as wedding cakes), and rich with the brown butter and tender apples.

This is the only dish in this chapter that I'm not giving you a scaled-down recipe for. It's a big one – a cake for a wedding or a big celebration. It will take a decent number of hours across a couple of days. But that's the thing about a wedding cake. If you're making one for someone (or even for yourself), it's all about sharing your love. And so it's worth taking time over.

CARAMEL APPLE AND SAGE CAKE WITH BROWN BUTTER ICING

Serves 40 very generously, or cuts into 80 wedding portions

CARAMEL APPLES
300g (1½ cups) caster (superfine) sugar
50g (1¾oz) butter, diced
10 Bramley (cooking) apples, peeled,
  cored and cut into cubes

CAKE
700g (1lb 9oz) butter
750g (1lb 10oz) light brown sugar
10 eggs
1kg (2lb 4oz) plain (all-purpose) flour

300g (10½oz) sour cream
55g (2oz) baking powder
5tsp ground cinnamon
2tsp ground cardamom
2tsp ground ginger
20g (¾oz) sage leaves, finely shredded
A large pinch of salt

CRYSTALLIZED APPLE
3 crisp eating apples
200g (1 cup) granulated sugar

BROWN BUTTER BUTTERCREAM
1.8kg (4lb) unsalted butter
680g (1lb 8oz) egg whites*

1.2kg (2lb 10oz) caster (superfine) sugar
1½tsp salt
1tsp cream of tartar
4tsp vanilla bean paste

TO DECORATE
Fresh sage

EQUIPMENT
15cm (6in) and 20cm (8in) cake pans,
    ideally loose-bottomed or springform
Cake boards and dowelling
A mixer or stick blender (you can make
    the icing by hand, but I wouldn't
    recommend it)

*I buy a carton of egg whites, rather than separating individual eggs

Some tips:
• You'll need at least two shelves in your fridge, so make some space in advance.
• This seems like so much icing, I know. But the last thing you want is to be
panicking about quantities when spreading it over the final cake. Plenty of
icing means you can be generous between layers, and still have spare to fix any
accidents.

DAY ONE

1. For the caramel apples, stir together the caster sugar and 150ml
(scant ⅔ cup) water in a saucepan, then bring to a simmer over a
moderate heat. Cook the caramel until a rich golden brown, then stir
in the diced butter. Whisk until the caramel is pale and smooth. Add
the apples and cook until soft. When you add them and they first start
to release liquid, the caramel will clump and stretch and you'll be
convinced you've somehow ruined it. Don't panic. It will melt down
again. You're adding too much liquid in the apples for it to be as thick
and rich as it was, but you're doing this for the caramel flavour. Set
aside to cool.

2. Preheat the oven to 160°C/315°F/Gas 2–3 and grease and line both cake pans. My mixer isn't big enough for all this cake batter (and I don't have duplicate cake pans), so I do the cakes in two batches: one large and one small, then the same again. If you're planning to do the same, follow steps 3–5 twice, with half the cake ingredients each time.

3. Cream together the butter and light brown sugar until the mixture is light, and no longer feels grainy when you rub a pinch between your fingertips. Beat in the eggs, along with a few tablespoons of the flour, and then the sour cream. Fold in the rest of the flour, the baking powder, spices, sage and salt.

4. Scoop the apples out of the now runny caramel, and fold them into the cake batter. (Keep the leftover caramel to pour over pancakes or ice cream.)

5. Split the cake batter between the cake pans, and bake the cakes until risen and springing back when prodded; a skewer inserted should come out clean. The smallest should take 50 minutes, and the larger just over an hour. Ensure you don't open the oven door for at least the first 35 minutes, to prevent the cakes from sinking. Once cooked, let cool for 10 minutes in their pans, then turn out onto wire racks to cool completely. As soon as the cakes are cool, wrap them in plastic wrap, so they don't dry out.

6. While the cakes are baking, make the brown butter for the icing. Cut the butter into large chunks and put it in a saucepan over a moderate heat. Once foaming, turn the heat down and keep cooking until rich hazelnut brown flecks have collected in the bottom of the pan. The butter will smell deliciously nutty. This is a lot of butter, so you don't want to burn it; as soon as you suspect it might have gone far enough, take it off the heat and tip it into a cold bowl to stop it cooking. You can always put it back in the pan to cook some more if you like. Cover the browned butter and put in the fridge to solidify.

DAY TWO

1. Make the icing. Bring the brown butter out of the fridge – you should have about 1.6kg (scant 3lb 8oz) now. Leave it to soften, it should be about 16°C (61°F) when you add it to the meringue, so don't let it melt but you should be able to spoon it very easily.

2. Put the egg whites, sugar, salt and cream of tartar in a large heatproof bowl and place over a pan of simmering water. Stir constantly with a whisk or spatula until the mixture reaches 85°C (185°F). Take off the heat, and beat on a moderate speed to stiff peaks, speeding up once the meringue has turned white and pillowy. Keep beating until the bowl cools; this will take up to 15 minutes. If you rush this step, the butter will melt rather than being beaten in – your meringue needs to be about 21°C (70°F) when you start adding the butter.

3. If you're using a mixer, switch to a paddle attachment. Start adding the softened brown butter, a tablespoon at a time, beating on a medium speed. The icing will deflate and become a bit lax and soupy at some point, but have faith – it will thicken up again. Once thick and holding stiff peaks, beat in the vanilla. Set the icing aside.

4. To make the crystallized apples, slice the apples finely through the core with a mandoline or sharp knife. Bring the granulated sugar and 250ml (1 cup) water to a simmer over a low heat. Once the sugar has dissolved, drop the apple slices in. Simmer for 15 minutes, then pull the slices out with tongs and place on a lined baking tray. Place in a 160°C/315°F/Gas 2–3 oven for 20 minutes, until a rich caramel brown. Set aside to harden.

5. Slice each of the four cakes into three layers. You may need to take a shelf out of your fridge – the cakes will be tall once you stack them. Start by placing the top piece of one of the larger cakes (trim it if it has domed a little) on the larger cake board. Spread with a generous layer

of icing, then add the other layers, with icing between them. Trim the top of the other larger cake if it has domed, and stack it on top, so you have a six-tier cake. Once the layers are assembled, apply a 'crumb coat': a thin layer of icing to keep crumbs out of the final layer of icing. Place in the fridge for an hour to firm up. Do the same to stack the smaller cakes, on their own cake board.

6. Once firmed up, remove each cake from the fridge and spread a thicker layer of icing over each one, smoothing it out or keeping it a little more 'casual', depending on your taste. Make sure you've covered the edge of the cake board with icing too, to hide it. It's now time to assemble.* Once the layers are iced, measure the dowelling against the side of the larger cake, trimming the sticks so they will lie flush with the top of the icing. Push at least three pieces of dowelling into the bottom layer, and then (take a deep breath) drop the smaller cake on top. Decorate with the sage and the crystallized apple slices.

7. To serve, split each large cake through the centre (so you have four three-tiered cakes), then cut into straight lengths, and then slice each length into fingers. You'll get at least 80, with icing-rich off-cuts to feast on the next day.

*If your cake is going to have to sit around all day, as it will at a wedding, find supports that feel right for you. For weddings, we use bamboo dowels and silver single-use cake boards. Everything will be masked and hidden, but you'll be much more easily able to lift the layers off to slice them up, and they won't sink into each other as the day goes on.

'Yeah,' she said. 'I want to marry you. I've always wanted to marry you. I just… it never occurred to me that we could. That we didn't need anyone's approval.'

'We don't,' I said.

'Then I do.'

I laughed and sat up in our bed. I turned on the light on my nightstand. Celia sat up, too. We faced each other and held hands.

The Seven Husbands of Evelyn Hugo, Taylor Jenkins Reid

I have to be honest with you as we come to a close in this chapter on weddings: it's tricky to find good ones in literature. Not good in terms of dramatic weight or memorable writing, but deeply *good*, those worthy of emulating. There's no shortage of iconic moments: Miss Havisham in her moth-eaten wedding dress with a mouldy cake in the corner, Jane Eyre's wedding to Rochester interrupted by some deeply unwelcome news regarding those noises in the attic, Lola marrying her rapist as Briony watches on in *Atonement*, the intricate family dynamics to take into account in *Cassandra at the Wedding*, Tita weeping into the wedding cake batter and making everyone sick in *Like Water for Chocolate*, the literal blood-bath that is George R. R. Martin's famous Red Wedding. Even some of the weddings I've referred to in the pages preceding this one – the alcohol-fuelled mess that is the wedding in *Seating Arrangements*, the devastating arranged marriage in *The Mercies* – are less than ideal. As iconic as these moments are, they're not weddings that should serve as inspiration.

It's hardly surprising, of course. Conflict is at the core of storytelling. And so, when the wedding is conflict-free – a happy ending – it tends to happen off the page. The double wedding in *Pride and Prejudice* that we see at the end of the BBC adaptation doesn't happen on the page; we hear only that there is a day when Mrs Bennet 'gets rid of her two most deserving daughters' (sorry Kitty). Peter Wimsey and Harriet Vane tie the knot in *Busman's Honeymoon*, but we read about it only in his mother's diary – she grudgingly admits, to her surprise, that their wedding breakfast was 'very good'. There is no elaborate breakfast for Meg March and Mr Brooke's nuptials, but we read of fruit, cake, flowers and lemonade. Anne Elliot and patient Captain Wentworth eventually marry, in *Persuasion*, but their wedding is anticipated in one paragraph and their life 'settled' the next.

There's an episode of *Sex and the City* in which Carrie is walking furiously down a Manhattan street, railing against the celebration gap – that reality that if you're an unmarried, childless person, there just aren't opportunities for your life milestones to be celebrated in a meaningful way. There are few moments in our adult lives where we can convince our social circle to travel to us en masse to stay in hotels, to do some group dancing, to accept a seating plan that places us next to an overly effusive aunt. I struggle, perhaps unsurprisingly given my mostly single twenties, with our relentless societal focus on marriage as the pinnacle. And so I suppose I quite relish the trickier narratives, the delicious horror of them.

And yet.

Occasionally we're let in, to observe small moments of wedding bliss. Celia and Evelyn deciding to marry in their bed one night in *The Seven Husbands of Evelyn Hugo*, despite not (legally) being able to. A swim and then fish and chips and Champagne in the pub garden in *Tin Man*. Sophie reckoning that she and Howl (he of the *Moving Castle*) 'ought to live happily ever after'. Eilis and Tony in *Brooklyn*, marrying at City Hall and celebrating with hot dogs at Coney Island.

Happy All the Time's Vincent and Misty going home to eat dinner in bed together after their small ceremony. They're wedding moments that have planted themselves in my memory, even if they've not been right for the recipes in these pages.

Because here's the last thing, the true thing. I love weddings. *Love* them. I'm a big romantic, a weepy, sentimental old fool. When I work at weddings – serious, high pressure, physically intense work – I still manage to find myself, at every single one, with a lump in my throat, my glassy eyes reflecting the harsh lights of our marquee kitchen. A stoic I am not. That our couples (that is how I always think of them – our couples) have filled halls and fields and gardens with their best people, have brought them together to witness the declaration of love they are making out loud, is moving in a way that feels new every time. I'm a sucker, you see, for a happy ending. Even if – no spoilers for any of the fictional ones above – it's often only temporary.

HOUSE
PARTIES

They talked about the Telegraph Club for a few minutes – or Kath and Sal did, while Lily sipped her drink and tried to pretend as if she went to these sorts of parties all the time. Over in the corner by the record player she saw two women laughing, one woman's arms looped around the other's neck as if they were about to start dancing.

Last Night at the Telegraph Club, Malinda Lo

I have a special and abiding affection for the bit of a party that is technically actually 'getting ready beforehand'. In my teens it was the part of the night during which I felt least self-conscious, before everything descended into a crowded chaos I was never quite relaxed enough to enjoy. Now that we're not sixteen anymore and we're more likely to be getting ready solo, it's a vanishingly rare thing to do. What a true tragedy. I long always to be getting dolled up in the company of my nearest and dearest, doing each other's hair, handing over a favourite lipstick, laying thick a blanket of compliments and adoration that will keep us warm all evening. I love, too, the way in which this sort of getting ready turns us back into teenagers all over again, brushing off the news that someone we've been lusting over might be in attendance, teasing each other over blush-pink cheeks.

That's the other thing about a house party that is so glorious, you see. The thrill of possibility it offers in terms of who you might see. Without the restriction of a table or a seating plan between you, there's always a chance that you'll catch someone's eye across the room, that that woman you (I) can't stop thinking about will show up looking devastatingly gorgeous, that you'll find yourselves knocking shoulders with them by the drinks lined up between the toaster and the sink. And if you do, it's all to play for. It's possible to get away with things in a crowd that would carry too much weight elsewhere. Dinners and dates are all well and good, but the haze of a good party is the best place in the world to flirt.

It is hardly surprising, then, that house parties are where so much of the best and most delicious courting/flirting/kissing in literature happens. Jane Austen set some of her most compelling scenes at house parties – the night at Netherfield when Darcy and Elizabeth finally dance, the London party where Marianne is rebuffed by Willoughby, the ball at which Emma watches Mr Knightley ask Harriet, left without a partner, to join him on the floor. Meg March later relays to Jo that at Sallie Moffat's party she drank Champagne and flirted and 'was altogether abominable'. Jay Gatsby's parties are merely a thinly veiled excuse to bring his beloved Daisy back into his orbit. Jilly Cooper's parties (in *Harriet*, in *Rivals*, in literally every one of her perfect, party-filled, novels) allow her characters to flirt, to fight, to pose, to exert their power. Love-struck Zami watches Muriel circulating with ease at Nicky and Joan's stuffy New Year's Eve party, and finds that feeding their hungover friends at an impromptu recovery party the next night suits her much better. The delightfully debaucherous Regency balls in Lex Croucher's *Reputation*. The Feddens' 25th wedding anniversary in *The Line of Beauty*, fuelled by Champagne and cocaine, sees everyone dance with Mrs Thatcher (and Nick head upstairs for a threesome). Lily watches all the women dance together in *Last Night at the Telegraph Club*, and longs to join them. Dressed as a stuffed olive, *Angus, Thongs and Full-Frontal Snogging's* Georgia Nicolson is mostly ignored by her peers and then dances solo in the living room. Henry can't help but kiss Alex on New Year's in *Red, White & Royal Blue*, after jealously watching him dance and flirt with everyone else all evening.

A party will helpfully assemble all the characters like chess pieces, playing them off against one another, manoeuvring them in precisely the right direction. The plot turns on these parties, on everything that is set up or followed through within them. In real life, things are rarely quite so narratively satisfying. But the promise of running into that person you've been thinking about? The thought of that perfect party playing out just the way you hope? The possibilities are delicious.

Reading *Zami: A Spelling of My New Name*, I was thrilled by the description of a table laid for a party. Alongside crudités, caviar, pretzels and mixed nuts is a bowl of sour cream and onion dip, made from Lipton's onion soup mix. Growing up in Australia it was a staple, but I hadn't eaten it in years.

The original recipe is, literally, child's play. You simply open a sachet of onion soup mix and stir it through a tub of sour cream. If your family are so inclined, you might chop some chives over the top. But finding the right soup mix twenty-five years later has been a series of disappointments. You might be luckier than me, but I have instead taken to putting together my own from my spice cupboard. Don't skip the MSG here (look in east Asian supermarkets or online) – it's the real flavour hero. When I first put out a dish of this for friends, it was described as a dip that tastes exactly like crisps. Which is precisely what it is.

SOUR CREAM AND ONION DIP

Makes a good-sized bowl for a party

2tbsp dried onion flakes
1tsp dried thyme
1tsp garlic powder
½tsp dried mustard powder
½tsp flaky sea salt

⅛tsp MSG
⅛tsp black pepper
600ml (scant 2½ cups) sour cream
Plenty of chopped chives, to serve

1. Mix together the dry ingredients, then stir through the sour cream. Taste – this is a personal thing; you might need more heat from mustard, garlic or black pepper, or more salt to bring it all to life.

2. Top with the chopped chives, and serve alongside plenty of crudités and some corn chips.

If, however, you're planning on buying some dips to serve alongside (or instead of) the sour cream and onion, I heartily recommend you tart them up a little (like all of us before a party, a pot of dip could always use a bit of a zhuzh). Allow me to offer some ideas:

The smoothest supermarket **hummus** is lovely swirled onto a plate, and dressed with some **good olive oil** and **dukkah**, or **a big pinch of ground paprika**. Serve with **salted crisps**.

A tub of **taramasalata** spooned into a flat bowl can be topped with **a tablespoon of capers** fried in **a tablespoon of olive oil** until crisp. Eat with squidgy fingers of **focaccia**.

Tzatziki from a pot is even better if you stir through some **chopped dill**. Fry some **cumin and coriander seeds** in a tablespoon of **butter** until the butter just starts to brown, and pour it over the top. Brilliant with **crunchy crudités**.

Top **baba ganoush** with a swirl of **tahini**, a handful of **toasted pine nuts**, and lots of **coriander leaves**. Serve it alongside some **flat bread or pita**.

The other Australian classic from my childhood was sweet chilli sauce stirred through cream cheese. Nowadays, I prefer something a little sharper; try whisking **a tablespoon of gochujang paste**, **a teaspoon of rice vinegar** and **a teaspoon of honey** through **a 180g (6oz) tub of cream cheese**. Cream cheese is thick, so it needs something robust for dipping, like **rice crackers or crisps**.

At Cecilia's party, the first and last one that the Lisbon sisters are allowed to host in *The Virgin Suicides*, everyone stands around awkwardly sipping punch. Though there's nothing else about this party I'd wish to emulate, the image of that 70s punch bowl has stayed with me. In truth, this recipe is at least partially motivated by knowing that I'd have an excuse to buy a proper punch bowl, perhaps one with little glasses hanging from it. This retro sophistication contrasts starkly with a horribly memorable punch from my teenage years: a plastic bin filled with everyone's booze, spiked with blue food dye that then stained everyone's mouths.

The joy of this punch is that it's just as good without the rum as it is with it. There are more and more non-drinkers in my life, so it's always in the back of my mind to keep the alcohol-free drinks as exciting and delicious as the boozy ones. Keep the punch itself virgin, and place a bottle alongside for people to spike their own. It allows you to cater to all your guests without needing to buy a second punch bowl.

SUMMER PUNCH

Makes enough for 12

SHRUB*

300g (10½oz) peaches, stones removed
150g (5½oz) honey
150g (¾cup) caster (superfine) sugar
1tsp peppercorns
300ml (1¼cups) white wine vinegar

PUNCH

400g (14oz) green seedless grapes
400g (14oz) red seedless grapes
50g (1¾oz) fresh mint, leaves picked
4 limes
500ml (generous 2 cups) apple juice
750ml (3 cups) fiery ginger beer
750ml (3 cups) sparkling water
Golden rum (optional)

*A shrub is usually made without heat (the fruit macerating in the sugar for a couple of days, adding vinegar, and then straining it). But I want to give you a faster option. Heat speeds up the process, so you can have a shrub in the time it takes your grapes to freeze solid. Drink the rest of the bottle with sparkling water.

1. First, prepare the shrub. Use a potato masher to squash the peach flesh in a small saucepan. Add the honey, sugar and peppercorns and place over a moderate heat. Once the sugar has melted, squash everything around again and then set aside in the saucepan for 3–4 hours.

2. Meanwhile, pull the grapes from their stems, tip into a bag and place in the freezer for at least 4 hours.

3. Add the vinegar to the peach and sugar, stirring it through. Strain through a fine sieve. Pour into a sterilized bottle and store in the fridge. It will keep for at least a month like this.

4. To make the punch, pull the mint leaves from their stems, and slice the limes into thin rounds before pulling out any seeds.

5. Pour 150ml (scant ¾ cup) shrub into a punch bowl (or a large jug) and add the mint leaves. Bash about a little with the handle of a wooden spoon, then add the lime slices.

6. Top up with the apple juice, ginger beer and sparkling water. Taste before serving – it should be sharp, sweet, sour and refreshing. Add the frozen grapes, to keep everything cold without diluting it. Add a splash (or more) of rum, if you like. As the party progresses, you may need to add some ice to your glasses.

There are few books quite as good as Michael Cunningham's *The Hours*. Three narratives overlay each other within it: Virginia Woolf is struggling with her novel and her mental health; Clarissa Vaughan is planning a party for her friend Richard; Mrs Brown is suffering through an unhappy marriage. Across the twentieth century, the three women are all linked thanks to their respective relationships with that other perfect party book: Woolf's classic *Mrs Dalloway*.

The party that Clarissa has been planning does not happen as she had intended, but the food is laid out regardless. There's a crab casserole, Richard's favourite, which is compelling, but which I imagine isn't particularly easy to serve while you have a glass in hand. Otherwise, it's ideal finger food for a party: steamed shrimp, griddled chicken breast on skewers, miniature onion tarts, round sandwiches, goat's cheese and walnuts smeared onto endive leaves, squares of rare tuna with wasabi, and triangles of grilled aubergine.

RARE TUNA WITH WASABI

Makes 40 squares

60g (½ cup) toasted sesame seeds
2tsp shichimi tōgarashi*
3tbsp sesame oil

400g (14oz) fresh tuna, cut into slices at least 2cm (¾in) thick
3tbsp mayonnaise (Kewpie if you have it)
Wasabi, to taste

*A Japanese spice blend made from a combination of chilli, sanshō, orange zest, hemp seeds, black and white sesame seeds, poppy seeds, nori and ginger. Lots of supermarkets stock it now, but you can find it online if not.

1. Mix the sesame seeds and tōgarashi together in a flat bowl. Pour the sesame oil into another flat dish.

2. Pat the tuna dry with some paper towels. Dip it into the sesame oil, then into the sesame seed mix. Press down to ensure you have good coverage, then flip over and repeat on the other side.

3. Heat a dry pan over a moderate heat. Once searingly hot, place the tuna in the pan. Cook for a minute on one side, then flip over carefully (trying not to knock the sesame seeds) and cook for another minute on the other side. Remove the tuna from the pan and place onto a clean board.

4. With a sharp knife (you want your cuts to be clean and neat), cut the tuna into squares, with seeds on the top and bottom, and transfer to a serving plate.

5. Mix the mayonnaise and wasabi – taste it as you add the wasabi – then pipe or smear a little onto the top of each tuna square. Serve while still warm.

GRILLED AUBERGINE WITH ROMESCO

Makes about 40 canapés

3 aubergines (eggplants), tops removed, cut lengthways into slices 5mm (¼in) thick
100ml (scant ½ cup) good olive oil
6 sprigs of dill
Sea salt

ROMESCO
100g (¾ cup) whole almonds

200g (7oz) chargrilled red (bell) peppers from a jar
1 garlic clove
1tsp hot paprika
2tsp sherry vinegar
Up to 2tbsp olive oil

EQUIPMENT
Cocktail sticks

1. Place the aubergine slices in a colander or sieve, sprinkle generously with salt and leave for 10 minutes while you make the romesco filling.

2. Toast the almonds in a dry pan until starting to brown on the outside. Blitz with the drained peppers in a food processor or using a stick blender. Add the garlic, paprika and vinegar and blitz again. Add the olive oil, a little at a time (how much you need will depend

on how oily your peppers were when they went in); the sauce should have good body, like a thick jarred pesto. Taste and season with salt.

3. Pat your aubergine slices dry. Paint the slices with the olive oil, and then place in a dry pan over a moderate heat (you will need to do this in batches). You want to get some good colour on both sides, but don't let them crisp up as you want to be able to roll them. Remove from the pan, and slice in half lengthways on the diagonal. Repeat with the rest of the aubergine.

4. Once the aubergine slices have cooled to room temperature (too hot and the romesco will run everywhere), place a teaspoon of the sauce and a couple of fronds of dill at the wide base of the triangle of aubergine and then roll up towards the point. Push a cocktail stick through the aubergine to seal it. They can be stored in the fridge at this point, but bring them out an hour before serving.

Bang bang chicken is such a tempting title for a dish that it is hardly surprising that there are so many different versions of it. In Sichuan, where the dish originated, the chicken is poached, hammered so that it can be torn apart (hence the bang bang) and served with a spicy, zesty sauce. I make Fuchsia Dunlop's recipe for it regularly, and it's unsurprisingly glorious.

But in the US, bang bang chicken is often fried rather than poached, then topped with a spiced mayonnaise. And so, at the anniversary party near the beginning of Zadie Smith's *On Beauty*, when Kiki carries bang bang chicken out of the kitchen on a canapé platter, I'm willing to put money on it being more like this version below. Crisp, moreish, easy to eat with a glass in hand – it tastes great with the 'very good bottle' of Champagne Kiki collects from the fridge alongside it. I've swapped the mayonnaise I first imagined for a sauce inspired by Hetty McKinnon's broccoli noodles (which I'm obsessed with) – whisking water into sesame paste and chilli oil changed my life.

BANG BANG CHICKEN

Makes 40 canapé-sized pieces

750g (1lb 10oz) chicken thigh fillets
½tsp ground white pepper
½tsp garlic powder
½tsp caster (superfine) sugar
½tsp ground Sichuan peppercorns
A pinch of salt
1tbsp black sesame vinegar
1tbsp soy sauce
1 egg
2 litres (2 quarts) vegetable oil
200g (2 cups) cornflour (cornstarch)

3tbsp sesame seeds

SAUCE
1tsp ground Sichuan peppercorns
4tbsp Chinese sesame paste, or tahini
1tbsp soy sauce
2tbsp chilli oil
2tsp black sesame vinegar
1tbsp sesame oil
A pinch of salt

1. Place the meat between two sheets of greaseproof paper, and take

to your chicken thighs with a mallet or a rolling pin. You want them flattened to about 1cm (½in) thick and tenderized, but don't bash them to pieces. Slice each flattened thigh into chunks.

2. In a bowl, prepare a marinade with the white pepper, garlic powder, sugar, Sichuan peppercorns, salt, vinegar, soy sauce and egg. Whisk together well, then add the chicken, turning it over and over with your hands to coat. Set aside for an hour outside of the fridge (make sure it's somewhere cool if it's a hot day). Alternatively, if it's easier, you can leave the chicken in its marinade in the fridge overnight.

3. Prepare the sauce by whisking all the ingredients together with 1 tablespoon water until smooth. Another tablespoon of water might be necessary if it's a bit too thick for drizzling.

4. Heat the oil to 180°C/350°F in a deep-sided saucepan. If you don't have a thermometer, place the handle of a wooden spoon in; when the oil is hot enough, streams of little bubbles should issue from it. Tip the cornflour and sesame seeds into a flat bowl, and toss the chicken through it in batches. Fry for 4 minutes until golden and crisp, then drain on paper towels.

5. Once all the chicken has been cooked, check the temperature of the oil again; bring it back up to 180°C/350°F if it's dropped. Fry the chicken again for a final minute, again in batches. Place on a serving plate, season with a little salt, then spoon some of the sauce onto each piece. Serve with toothpicks so people can spear their own.

The 'longest and most destructive party' in literature is probably still going. When Douglas Adams wrote about it in *Life, the Universe and Everything*, it was already in its fourth generation. So ruinous is it that it has destroyed entire cities that sit on the planet beneath it, raided for avocado dip, spare ribs, drinks and cheese crackers in order to satisfy the guests.

They would need to be *very* good party nibbles. But, of course, cheese crackers are. They used to be a favourite after-school snack, spread with butter and Vegemite and eaten in a little stack with a cup of tea. This version owes a lot to my friend Liv's Parmesan sables; we often top them with a smear of goat's cheese and a bit of chutney for weddings. But when rolled out more thinly, they crisp up beautifully and are great for snacking on with a beer or glass of fizz in your hand – salty and fiery and satisfying.

CHEESE CRACKERS

Makes at least 80

200g (1½ cups) plain (all-purpose) flour
¼tsp salt
½tsp mustard powder
½tsp cayenne pepper

A pinch of ground black pepper
100g (3½oz) butter, cold from the fridge
150g (5½oz) Cheddar cheese, grated
50g (1¾oz) Parmesan, grated

1. This is a job for a food processor, if you have one; just dump all the ingredients into it, then blitz until the mixture starts to come together into a dough. If you don't, put the flour, salt, mustard, cayenne and black pepper in a bowl, then rub the butter in with your fingertips. Mix through the grated cheeses, then bring the dough together.

2. Cover the dough, or wrap in plastic wrap, and rest in the fridge for at least 30 minutes.

3. Preheat the oven to 190°C/375°F/Gas 5. Lay out two sheets of

greaseproof paper and put a quarter of the dough between them. Roll it out thinly; not so thin that you can see through the cracker, but no more than a millimetre thick. Cut small circles or squares out of the dough, squidging it back together and rolling out again when necessary. Place the crackers on a lined baking sheet and transfer to the oven for 6–7 minutes, until golden around the edges.

4. Cool on the baking sheet for a couple of minutes while you cut out the next batch. Transfer to a wire rack to cool completely before storing in an airtight container. They'll stay crisp for up to a week, but are best when fresh.

I have written recipes for sausage rolls before. There was one in the Midnight Feasts chapter of my first book – the version my granny makes, laced with Worcestershire sauce and hot English mustard. There's a mushroom, leek and miso version in the Cocktail Parties chapter of my Christmas book. And here we are again, with more sausage rolls – this time made sweet and salty with mango chutney (an inspired Liv addition) and soy sauce.

The truth is, I couldn't very well write a book about parties in which they were absent, an impulse reinforced by the books on my shelves. Our titular heroine in Jilly Cooper's *Prudence* joins Mrs Braddock to make them for Lucasta's birthday party. They're part of the complicated 'beige feast' at the Christmas Eve party in Juno Dawson's *Stay Another Day*. In *Once, Twice, Three Times an Aisling*, a list of Mandy's favourite canapés has sausage rolls on top (naturally). Neville takes a sausage roll off a platter during a big party that brings the Cazalets together in Elizabeth Jane Howard's *Casting Off*. Sausage rolls are part of the spread when Adrian Mole and his neighbours celebrate the Royal Wedding with a street party. They're ubiquitous, they're delicious. They're perfect.

SAUSAGE ROLLS

Makes around 64 little rolls

2 brown onions, finely diced
1 carrot, grated
2 crisp eating apples, grated
500g (1lb 2oz) sausage meat*
500g (1lb 2oz) minced (ground) pork, at
   least 10 per cent fat
125g (4½oz) soft white breadcrumbs
6tbsp mango chutney

2tbsp soy sauce
1tbsp cider vinegar
Lots of freshly ground black pepper
A large pinch of flaky sea salt
1 egg
4 sheets ready-rolled puff pastry
1tbsp sesame seeds

*I squeeze the meat from a packet of good sausages – the texture and seasoning give your sausage rolls a good kickstart.

1. In a mixing bowl, bring together the onions, carrot, apples, meat, breadcrumbs, mango chutney, soy sauce, vinegar, and seasoning. Squidge everything together with your hands.

2. Whisk the egg in a small bowl and set aside. Preheat your oven to 200°C/400°F/Gas 6. Lay out a sheet of pastry, with the narrower end parallel to the edge of your work surface. Slice in half, again parallel to the edge of the work surface. On each half, place ⅛ of the filling in a line along the longer edge. The line of filling should be a generous 2cm (¾in) high.

3. Roll the pastry tightly over the meat. Paint some of the beaten egg along the top edge of the pastry, then roll the meat over it to seal. Paint the roll with more beaten egg, then slice each roll into eight pieces (a bread knife or serrated knife is the best one to use here) and transfer to a lined baking sheet. They will puff up, so give them a little space. Sprinkle the tops with sesame seeds. Repeat with the remaining pastry and filling.

4. Bake to a deep golden colour; 25–30 minutes should do it. Allow to cool slightly before serving, or serve at room temperature if you prefer.

If they told us to come over and talk to them, we tried to sparkle in conversation. Some treated us like adults, others laughed at us when we were not meaning to be funny. When they needed an ashtray, another drink, when they wanted to know where the pans were because they had decided to fry eggs at three a.m., Ingrid and I fought each other for the job.

Sorrow and Bliss, Meg Mason

Like Martha and Ingrid in *Sorrow and Bliss*, my first parties, the first ones I remember, were the parties hosted by my mum. She is as enthusiastic about having people around as I am, as passionate about being the hostess, as committed to covering the dining table with good things to eat. I grew up in a house with fifty of those incredibly nineties white porcelain canapé spoons in the cupboard. As a teenager I knew how to carefully polish the hired glasses (the ones that came free with the wine), had worked out the physical logistics of hauling three 5kg bags of ice back up the road from the service station, and could 'sparkle in conversation' with all the adults. It was the best possible training for the exact sort of adult I've become.

My first parties then, the first ones I hosted, happened once I moved to London. The first flat I lived in was a good one for house parties – small bedrooms but sweeping wide hallways that we utilized as common space and some outdoor space in the form of a huge flat roof atop the Lloyds Bank next door. The booze we drank was cheap, and the food was even cheaper – everyone showed up with bags of crisps and dips, and we'd head out for chips and garlic sauce from the kebab shop in the early hours. I'd make sausage rolls, occasionally, but the focus was more on the music and the flirting and the gin than it was the food. As a generally anxious person, I've had a complicated relationship with house parties. When I'm at my most anxious, the lack of a table between guests, of easily identifiable social conventions and rules, makes me retreat inside myself. In my twenties, I put on a good show of being a hostess. But I fear, in hindsight, that that's what it was: a performance, a role I was playing.

A decade or so on from those first parties in Whitechapel, the focus is still on the music and the flirting and the gin. But it is also now, undeniably, on the food. Whether it's because our hangovers are worse in our thirties, or simply that we're all much more interested in an excuse to gather together and eat something delicious, most house parties I find myself at are a sort of standing-up mismatched-plate potluck. It has made house parties an entirely different game. I can 'sparkle in conversation' with the adults, especially those I love, but it's a pleasure to be able to take on a little task when in the company of lots of people I don't know. As a guest I'll often poke my head into the kitchen to see if there's a job to do; when there's food on offer, there almost always is. At my own parties, it's where I spend most of my time, knowing that people will come and find me there.

And then I really come into my own in the early hours of the morning. When people are hungry, when they've kicked off their shoes and collapsed onto sofas, when someone starts mumbling about pizza even though all our culinary delivery options have long closed, I love to be able to present a solution. I usually have the wherewithal to, at the very least, find some toast and Vegemite. So that everyone wakes up feeling a bit better the next morning than we probably deserve to.

This is not really a recipe. A recipe implies preparation. A shopping trip to collect ingredients. Planning. This page is instead for when it's 3am and you're hungry. This is a not-quite-recipe for making do with what's at hand. A suggestion, if you will, for some eggs.

Martha and Ingrid, in Meg Mason's *Sorrow and Bliss*, point their mother's grown-up guests towards the frying pans and eggs when they're in need of late-night sustenance. It's my go-to plan too; of all the ingredients reliably available in my kitchen, eggs are king. They need so little of your time and your effort to be deeply satisfying.

EGGS AT 3AM

Gather up: **one or two eggs** per hungry guest, **some fat** (oil or butter), **bread** if you have any, and a frying pan

Frying an egg

You can fry your egg any way you like, of course, but I like a just-set white and a basically raw yolk. Heat a splash of oil or a knob of butter in the pan. Once hot, crack in as many eggs as you need. Add a tablespoon of water, and then pop some sort of lid over the pan – it doesn't matter if it's too big, you just want to let the steam cook the tops of the whites a little. Leave for a minute; if you fancy a jammy yolk rather than a runny one, cook it a little further. Serve with toast.

Variations

Add **a tin of anchovies** in their oil to the frying pan first, break them up a bit, then add **a knob of butter or extra teaspoon of oil** before you add your eggs.

Add **a couple of sage leaves** to the fat once it's hot, and move them around for a minute or two before you add the eggs. **Thyme** is good too, as is **rosemary**.

Add **a couple of tablespoons of jarred salsa** to one side of the pan, and then the oil and eggs on the other. Move the salsa around or it will stick and burn. Don't worry about putting the lid on here, just spoon the warm salsa over the egg once fried; it'll finish the white before it reaches your plate. I'm not going to call this *huevos rancheros*, because that title deserves better than this – not least a tortilla – but that's of course where this has its roots.

Add **a good teaspoon of capers** per egg to the hot fat, and move them around until they start to brown. Add **a generous pinch of chilli flakes** and then the eggs. Fry as before.

Add **a tablespoon of sauerkraut** to the egg in the pan instead of the water. Pop the lid on to steam as before – damp sauerkraut will help here.

The next step up from a fried egg is, I suppose, a slightly more fussy egg. In Eva Rice's gorgeous, party-filled *The Lost Art of Keeping Secrets*, Charlotte, Harry and Penelope have a 'Parisian breakfast' in the early hours of the morning. They dissect the events of the evening's party while sitting amidst the mess that remains of it. Their Parisian breakfast consists of omelettes – good, French ones I'll warrant. There is sparse detail in the text, but I want mine with cheese and with herbs, still slightly runny in the middle. The recipe below is for our Parisian breakfast trio; they'll need a fork each and a shared plate. If you want to serve more than three people, you'll need to make a couple of omelettes.

PARISIAN BREAKFAST (SOFT CHEESE OMELETTE)

Serves 3

5 medium eggs
1tsp chopped chives
1tsp chopped tarragon

50g (1¾oz) Comté cheese, finely grated
1tbsp unsalted butter
Salt and black pepper

1. Crack the eggs into a bowl and give them a really good whisk with a fork, until there are no remaining streaks of yolk or white. Season with a pinch of salt and pepper.

2. Place your chopped herbs, your grated cheese, your bowl of eggs, a fork (or spatula), and your serving plate close to the hob/stovetop. This will all be over in a matter of seconds, and you don't want to be dashing around trying to find anything.

3. Place your pan over a high heat and add the butter. Swirl the butter around so that the pan is well-greased, but don't let it brown. Tip the eggs in and leave for a couple of seconds, then start moving the pan around vigorously, as you stir the eggs with your fork (or a spatula if your pan is Teflon). Keep everything moving, until the bottom layer

starts to look set, but the top is still liquid. Sprinkle the herbs and cheese over the top.

4. Tip your pan at a 45-degree angle, allowing most of the (still runny) omelette to slip down to one edge. Fold the top half over the bulk of the omelette. Turn the heat off.

5. Grasp your pan handle in your dominant hand, with your thumb on top and palm below. Hold your plate in the other hand, almost vertically, then bring the pan up to meet it. Tip the omelette onto the plate – the set underside will become the top. Eat immediately, while it's still warm and at the point of runny inside.

Late at night, after performing onstage, *Tipping the Velvet*'s Kitty and Nan arrive home, where the after-party is in full swing. Sims, Percy and Tootsie are brewing tea and making hot chocolate, putting Welsh rabbit under the grill, and flipping pancakes on the stove. It sustains them through the game or songs that so often followed, before everyone found their way to bed before dawn.

Welsh rabbit/rarebit has a lengthy history; there are records of it as early as the eighteenth century. First published in 1747, Hannah Glasse's *The Art of Cookery* offers recipes for Scotch rabbit (toasted cheese), Welsh rabbit (cheese and mustard), and English rabbit (bread soaked in wine, topped with toasted cheese or a cheese sauce). It's the Welsh version that has persisted, incorporating some features of the others along the way. I like mine hot and fiery, so go hard on the cayenne and English mustard. Sub Henderson's Relish for the Worcestershire sauce for vegetarian guests.

WELSH RAREBIT

Makes 8 slices (for 4 or 8 of you)

3tbsp butter, plus extra for buttering
3tbsp plain (all-purpose) flour
400ml (1¾ cups) ale
300g (10½oz) mature Cheddar, grated

¼tsp cayenne pepper
1tsp English mustard powder
2tsp Worcestershire sauce
8 slices granary bread

1. First, make the sauce. Melt the butter in a saucepan and stir in the flour, then cook for at least 2 minutes. You're cooking the flour here, so don't rush to add the liquid. Add a splash of the ale and whisk through until the sauce is smooth, then continue to add the rest of the ale in stages. The sauce should be rich, but quite thin.

2. Stir in the grated cheese, cayenne, mustard powder and Worcestershire sauce. Cook the sauce until it is thick; it needs to stay on the toast while under the grill (broiler).

3. Heat your grill to high. Toast the bread until golden, either under the grill or in a toaster, and then butter. Lay all eight slices on a grill rack or lined baking sheet and divide the sauce between them. Put the rack/sheet under the grill and cook until the rarebit is bubbling and browned in patches. Keep an eye on it during this time; it's tempting to disappear to boil the kettle or pour someone a drink, but that's the moment that the toast will catch and burn and you'll set your fire alarm off. Leave for a minute before handing slices around; molten cheese will destroy the roof of your mouth.

It's late, it's freezing outside, and everyone is drunk and throwing around comments they might regret in the morning (this is Jilly Cooper's *Rivals* after all). Before Patrick's birthday cake is wheeled out, the guests sit around eating shepherd's pie and garlic bread. Rupert hunts for Taggie on the seating plan but she is, as ever, in the kitchen putting everything together. She's running around; all her helpers have vanished and there's no one to clear plates.

While I'm keen for us all to avoid ending up like Taggie, the dish itself is a great party choice. I'm not suggesting that you head off to the kitchen at 1am to start putting together a shepherd's pie. Instead, prep this in advance, then throw into the oven for 45 minutes before spooning out in generous portions, or simply attacking with forks.

SHEPHERD'S PIE

Serves 4–6 (double this recipe for a really generous vat of it)

3tbsp lard or light olive oil
500g (1lb 2oz) minced (ground) lamb – at least 20 per cent fat
1 large brown onion, finely diced
1 leek, finely diced
2 carrots, finely diced
2 celery sticks, finely diced
3 bay leaves
8 sprigs of thyme, leaves picked and finely chopped

2 garlic cloves, minced
400ml (1¾ cups) mushroom stock
2tsp Henderson's Relish or Worcestershire Sauce
250g (9oz) frozen peas
1.2kg (2lb 12oz) mashing potatoes
75g (5tbsp) butter, melted
50ml (3½tbsp) milk
Sea salt and black pepper

1. Warm half the fat in a saucepan over a moderate heat. Though it takes a little longer to brown the meat first, I can't advocate for it more enthusiastically – my mum always did it with any saucy minced meat dish she cooked. The end result will be richer and more delicious for it. Fry the lamb in a couple of batches until a deep brown, adding the rest of the fat when it's needed, then remove from the pan with a slotted spoon.

2. Add the onion and leek, and stir over a moderate heat for a couple of minutes until they start to lose their shape. Add the carrots and celery, and the bay leaves, and stir occasionally for 10 minutes, ensuring that the vegetables don't stick to the bottom of the pan. Add the garlic and thyme to the pan and cook for another couple of minutes.

3. Return the lamb to the pan, along with the stock. Turn the heat right down, put a lid on the pan and simmer for 45 minutes to an hour, stirring it every now and then. Once the sauce is thick and rich, add the Henderson's Relish and season to taste. It should be deeply savoury. Pick the bay leaves out, add the peas and stir through.

4. While the meat is cooking, peel the potatoes and chop into large chunks. Bring a large pot of salted water to the boil, and cook until a fork inserts easily into a potato. Drain into a colander and allow the potatoes to sit until they're as dry as possible.

5. Mash or push the potato through a potato ricer, then mix the melted butter and milk through the mash. Taste and season with more salt if you need it. Tip the meat into a roasting dish and then spoon the mash over the top. Smooth out and then scrape over the top with a fork. Cover and store in the fridge; it will last for a couple of days like this.

6. When you're ready to cook, preheat the oven to 180°C/350°F/ Gas 4 and bake for 40 minutes until the potato is golden brown on top. Serve immediately.

Casey McQuiston's *One Last Stop* is a party book. It's a love story between twenty-first century August and time-travelling Jane, who's been on the Q line of the New York subway for decades. But at heart it's about Agust and her found family. It's about brunch parties and late-night parties and train parties. It's about figuring out your place in the world and about a batch of pancakes that might save a diner.

Pancakes are a bit time consuming for a crowd, and short of owning endless frying pans and an industrial-sized cooker, there's no way to speed them up. So this is one to commit to when you have only a handful of friends left, a treat for the stragglers who stay to help you clean up. This base recipe will work with added blueberries, with chocolate chips or (as I'm suggesting here) alongside some crisp bacon, to honour Pancake Billy's House of Pancakes, and the strange magical time-travelling photo of Jane from 1976.

MIDNIGHT PANCAKES

Makes enough for 2–4

230g (1¾ cups) plain (all-purpose) flour
1tsp baking powder
½tsp bicarbonate of soda (baking soda)
A pinch of salt
40g (3tbsp) melted butter, plus extra for the pan
280ml (scant 1¼ cups) buttermilk
120ml (½ cup) milk

1 egg

TO SERVE
A couple of rashers (slices) of streaky bacon each
Butter
Maple syrup

1. Preheat your oven to its lowest possible setting. Sift the flour, baking powder, bicarbonate of soda and salt into a large mixing bowl and whisk the ingredients together.

2. In a separate bowl, combine the melted butter, buttermilk, milk and egg. Pour the wet ingredients into the dry and whisk to combine.

It's easy to over-mix this, so as soon as there are no large dry lumps in your batter, stop.

3. Heat a heavy-bottomed frying pan over a medium heat and add a small pat of butter to the pan. Once the butter is foaming slightly, ladle spoonfuls of the batter into the pan until pancakes form. Allow them to cook for a couple of minutes until bubbles have formed over the whole surface, then flip the pancakes and cook until the undersides are golden (less than a minute). Transfer to a baking sheet in the oven, until the batch is complete.

4. Meanwhile, cook your bacon. Layer the streaky rashers over the surface of a cold pan, then place over a low heat. To cook bacon that is crisp and even, rather than somehow both chewy and burnt, let it cook gradually, the fat rendering gently. Good bacon (the kind that doesn't leach water) will take about 12–15 minutes. It's not fast, I know, but let's face it – neither are your pancakes.

5. Let everyone assemble their own plate: thick fluffy pancakes, crisp bacon, a bit of melted butter and a generous pour of maple syrup.

... on Mondays eight servants, including an extra gardener, toiled all day with mops and scrubbing-brushes and hammers and garden-shears, repairing the ravages of the night before.

The Great Gatsby, F. Scott Fitzgerald

The first big house party I had a hand in planning was my eighteenth birthday. I still lived at home then, in the house I'd grown up in. The night ran exactly how I'd hoped – people clustered in groups outside; around buckets filled with ice and beer, hovering close to the fire as the temperature dropped.

But it's the next day I remember most clearly. We woke with a house still full of people – on sofas, top to tail on beds, on any patch of floor we could find. Mum scrambled eggs while the rest of us made our way through the debris, collecting empty glasses and bottles, discarded napkins, burst balloons. By the time brunch was on the table, we'd managed to return the house to some kind of equilibrium, the aftermath of the party gathered in bin bags and beer boxes that sat by the front door. We crowded in at the dining table, passing plates around, reliving favourite moments from the night before. Some dozen or so friends ended up staying for the day as we ate our way through party leftovers and snoozed in front of a forgettable run of Sunday afternoon films.

I still love the party clean up the morning after. I love the slightly hungover camaraderie of pulling things together, of everyone taking a role. I'm great at surfaces and sorting, my brother Tom and pal Tash are wizards at washing up, Ella returns a room to a cosy and comfortable state for us all to revel in. Anna brews the best pot of tea,

Bry will sort the recycling before you realise it needs to be done. I gather up the leftovers and sort the wheat from the chaff. This kind of clean-up is distinct from the sort that happens after a dinner party (where things are generally contained to the table and the kitchen), or a wedding (where you're less likely to be at home). House party cleaning is scrappy, and silly. I'll wonder how chairs have been upturned, how glasses ended up in rooms I was sure had closed doors; there's a joy in trying to piece together the narrative of the evening. Working out all those bits I missed.

To aid your cleaning efforts, add the biggest bin bags you can find to your shopping list, and make sure you have plenty of teabags and milk on hand – distributing mugs of strong milky tea in the morning will help get everyone started. And then, if I could offer one piece of advice, in those final minutes before you collapse into bed, it would be this: find a bowl, or a bucket, fill it with hot water and detergent, and drop any cutlery you can find into it. You'll be pleased you did. But otherwise, leave the aftermath until the morning after, when you can relish it.

He began walking home. He should have been exhausted but he felt energetic. Maybe Audra would be waiting for him with a bottle of wine. He would make turkey sandwiches and they would drink wine and discuss Thanksgiving, and she would say, as she did after every dinner party they had, 'On a scale of Delightful to Never Again, where would you rate it?'

Standard Deviation, Katherine Heiny

On a scale of Delightful to Never Again, where would you rate it? It's the perfect morning-after question – so delightfully prickly and human in a way that Katherine Heiny always nails in her novels. I've written throughout this book about my favourite parts of parties, about planning, and dressing up, about time in the kitchen, about laying out a huge spread, about the immediate aftermath. But before I bring everything to a close, before I wish you all the best in your parties to come, I want to speak with affection about the days to follow.

Parties are great, of course. But waking up cosy on a friend's sofa the next morning, making a pot of tea and a batch of bacon and egg rolls, and turning each part of the evening over as we come back to life, might be my very favourite part. During my teenage years, in those days of group calls on the home phone and MSN Messenger, I dreaded the morning after. I couldn't work out whether it was better to be spoken about or ignored entirely. My anxious little brain was always concerned by the things I may have done to set me apart from all those other girls who seemed to exist with a level of confidence

I could only dream of (they didn't, of course, but I didn't learn this until much later). As adults, propped up on pillows and beneath blankets, we chatter happily about how gorgeous everyone looked, pick apart that weird/fascinating/brilliant conversation we had with the people we were sitting next to at dinner, and poke at our sunburnt noses, aching feet and delicate heads. And, once the tea and rolls have brought us back to life, we inspect the fridge.

No matter how the party itself has gone, no matter who showed up (or didn't), regardless of any tensions you had to manage – and setting aside any last-minute culinary disasters – your fridge the next day will provide you with a rich bounty. While your party is technically over, the spoils remain.

When catering weddings, we always have a moment at about 10pm that we label the 'grab bag'. We clear out the hire fridges, and invite all our staff to lay their claim to pots of unused ingredients, piping bags full of creams and icing and plastic containers filled with leftovers. Everyone goes home with a slightly odd collection. But the thing is, quite apart from wanting to ensure nothing goes to waste, we know that when you've been working in the kitchen all day, the last thing you fancy doing when you get home is cooking.

I imagine you'll feel the same. And so I am pleased to point you towards things in the book that work well in their leftover state. I recommend the roast chicken (p71), stripped and stuffed into toasted sandwiches spread with gochujang-laced mayonnaise, or stirred through a bowl of packet ramen. Slices of the autumnal tart (p17) are lovely cold from the fridge, and respond particularly well to a smear of chutney or some pickled gherkins too. If you grilled too much aubergine (p160), warm the leftovers in a pan, fry some onions and a drained tin of chickpeas in olive oil with a pinch each of ground cumin and coriander, and toss the lot together before topping with feta and fresh herbs. The pork belly (p115) is lovely warmed up and served with sticky rice and some stir-fried greens. Poached salmon (p128) will be delightful in the poached salmon sandwiches (p14), or tossed at the last moment through a pasta sauce of sweated shallots, capers and sweet little cherry tomatoes. The romesco (p160) is good on pretty much everything, to be honest: with ricotta or an egg on toast, alongside some couscous and grilled vegetables, with soft creamy polenta, on anything crisp and fried. I'll regularly make a double batch to ensure I have enough for all of these in the week that follows an event. And this is before we start on the biscuits, parkin, panforte and wedding cake, all of which will be delicious the next day (so long as you remember to wrap them up or pop them in an airtight container – there's nothing sadder than a bone-dry wedding cake).

I wish delightful parties for you. Houses filled with loved ones, food you can't get enough of, plenty of ice in the freezer, a bit of dancing, a chance to flirt, gossip that keeps you sated in the days to come. But, at the very least, I wish you leftover sandwiches, and a great friend to dissect the madness of a Never Again party with afterwards.

RECIPE INDEX

READING INDEX

THANKS

I began this book during a pandemic. During the months alone, my skin itched with a need for company. There were bigger things going on. There still are. But what I most wanted was to host a dinner party. This book was a response to that want. These are the parties I most wanted to host, in those years when we couldn't.

Although I wrote this in isolation, I didn't make it in isolation. So. Some thank yous.

To Madeleine O'Shea, for making every sentence I write better, and for providing a space for me to write the books I want to write. To Jessie Price and to Clémence Jacquinet, for turning my words into the books that they are. I couldn't imagine more inspired and inspiring women to work with. To all at Head of Zeus, for being behind me in such a tangible way. To Zoe Ross, for your championing and for my career.

To Yuki Sugiura, for the beautiful photos, for your generous and glorious vision, for your openness and warmth. To Ella, for planning meetings, for making my food so beautifully, for being my other half. To Bry, for arriving with a suitcase full of props and a perfect eye. To Tom, for somehow always offering exactly what was needed. To Anna, for being such a lifeline in the planning and visualising.

To Chris, and Kim, for your gardens. To everyone else who came to chop veg, run to the shops, wash up, put your best dresses on, and flirt with each other: Andy, Berta, Dan, Hanni, Harriet, Jen, Jessie, Maddy, Nina, Rosa, Rosie, Pegi, and Tash.

To the novelists, for writing parties I want to be at. To the food writers who helped me realise these recipes – directly (to Rachel Roddy for talking lasagna and to Emiko Davies for talking artichokes) and indirectly (to those whose books I learn from and am inspired by. I tried to name you, and apologise wholeheartedly if I have failed – some of your food has been part of me for so long that I have forgotten it was yours first). To the food writers who supported *Christmas* so enthusiastically, especially Diana Henry, Caroline Eden, and Georgina Hayden. And to the friends who offered your recipes (to Fiona Zublin for your ginger nuts).

To everyone who tested the recipes (ate the recipes). I tried, and failed, to name you all. Please come to dinner soon.

To my beloved pals, who helped keep me sane through these 'unprecedented times', especially the Lockdown Outdoor Club, the RomCom Club, and You are AMAZING.

To my family on the other side of the world. For the party roadmap; for showing me how to make cocktails and slice finger sandwiches and prepare enough food for sixty. And to Luce, for learning alongside me.

To my family on this side of the world. For all the parties through the past decade and a half - the crayfish parties, the village hall birthdays and drunken Liverpool birthdays – for every Christmas Eve, and in anticipation of parties to come. And to Ingela, for hosting the sort of parties we still talk about.

To the Ashmans: Katya, Ben, and Tad, for the fact that being at your dining table feels like being at home, and for parties both sprawling and intimate around it.

To Liv Pollen. For a thousand ideas that were born in a kitchen we stood in together. And to the third in those kitchens as I was writing, Elly.

To Tash Hodgson, for opening the door after the plague. I wish always to be sitting beside you on the sofa, slightly hungover, with the FT and a bacon roll, the morning after.

And to Ella Risbridger, again. For your endless reassurance that this was the right book. For being my person on the end of the phone, for dreaming with me about the dinner parties we couldn't yet host, and for hosting them as soon as we could. Family family family.

EXTENDED COPYRIGHT

Extract from 'Aloeswood Incense' from *Love in a Fallen City* by Eileen Chang © 2007 by NYREV, Inc. Reprinted with permission from the New York Review of Books.

Bridget Jones' Diary © 1996 by Helen Fielding. Used with permission of Picador through PLSClear and Viking Books, an imprint of Penguin Publishing Group, a division of Penguin Random House LLC. All rights reserved.

Standard Deviation © 2017 by Katherine Heiny. Used by permission of Alfred A. Knopf, an imprint of the Knopf Doubleday Publishing Group, a division of Penguin Random House LLC (USA), and HarperCollins Publishers Ltd. All rights reserved.

The Remains of the Day © 1989 by Kazuo Ishiguro. Used by permission of Faber and Faber Ltd and Alfred A. Knopf, an imprint of the Knopf Doubleday Publishing Group, a division of Penguin Random House LLC. All rights reserved.

Crazy Rich Asians © 2013 by Kevin Kwan. Used by permission of Doubleday, an imprint of the Knopf Doubleday Publishing Group, a division of Penguin Random House LLC, and ICM Partners. All rights reserved.

The Lion, the Witch and the Wardrobe by C.S. Lewis © C.S. Lewis Pte Ltd 1950. Extract used with permission.

Last Night at the Telegraph Club © 2021 by Malinda Lo. Used by permission of Dutton Children's Books, an imprint of Penguin Young Readers Group, a division of Penguin Random House LLC. All rights reserved.

Looking For Alibrandi © Melina Marchetta 1992. Reprinted by permission of Jill Grinberg Literary Management LLC on behalf of the author.

Sorrow and Bliss by Meg Mason, copyright © 2020 by The Printed Page Pty Ltd. Reprinted by permission of Weidenfeld & Nicolson and HarperCollins Publishers Ltd.

One Last Stop © 2021 by Casey McQuiston. Reprinted by permission of St. Martin's Press.

Such a Fun Age © 2019 by Kiley Reid. Used by permission of G. P. Putnam's Sons, an imprint of Penguin Publishing Group, a division of Penguin Random House LLC, and Bloomsbury Publishing PLC (UK). All rights reserved.

The Seven Husbands of Evelyn Hugo by Taylor Jenkins Reid. Copyright © 2017 by Rabbit Reid, Inc. Reprinted with the permission of Atria Books, a division of Simon & Schuster, Inc., and Simon & Schuster UK. All rights reserved.

Extract from 'Potluck' from *Filthy Animals* © 2021 by Brandon Taylor. Used with permission of Daunt Books Publishing and Riverhead.

Cloudstreet ©Tim Winton 1991. Reprinted by permission of Jenny Darling & Associates on behalf of the author.